PRAISE FOR LISA MORTON'S NON-FICTION

Ghosts: A Haunted History

"In *Ghosts: A Haunted History*, Lisa Morton offers a compact account of the human propensity to believe in otherworldly apparitions. She discusses, among other matters, haunted houses, spiritualism, ghost-hunting, "Day of the Dead" and spectral terrors in literature, film and popular culture. To give body and shape to these phantoms and airy nothings, Morton packs her book with images — of paintings, creepy spirit photographs, movie stills and even a full-page illustration of Casper the Friendly Ghost...*Ghosts* abounds with phantasmic lore of every kind...the book reminds us that it's when the days are shortest and the nights darkest that we most need warmth and light and family. Paradoxically, it's at this same time of the year, and under just those cozy conditions, that we most enjoy spooky stories." Michael Dirda, *The Washington Post*, December 16, 2015

"Lisa Morton's brisk, handsomely illustrated *Ghosts: A Haunted History* canters through millennia of supposed uncanny interruptions with a kind of puckish scepticism . . . Morton excels at presenting us with instances of the persistence of belief, across all times and cultures..." – Jonathan Barnes, *The Times Literary Supplement*

"*Ghosts: A Haunted History* is intelligent and well structured, It's also well informed, which is apparent in the sheer volume of spectral examples that Morton has collected, yet her writing style remains accessible, and she doesn't allow the book to read like a jargon-heavy thesis...a perfect companion for those who err towards skepticism over embellishment, yet still find themselves riddled in goose-pimples when they hear a creak in the floorboards in the dead of night." – Richelle Charkot, *Rue Morgue* Magazine, December 2015

"*Ghosts* is brilliant, insightful and scary as hell. Lisa Morton proves that truth is definitely stranger than fiction." –Jonathan Maberry, New York Times bestselling author of *The Nightsiders* and *Ghostwalkers*

"In *Ghosts*, Lisa Morton brings her encyclopedic knowledge of folklore and the supernatural to bear on this vast, vital subject. For students of 'things that go bump in the night,' the book is simply indispensable." – Leslie S. Klinger, author of *The New Annotated H. P. Lovecraft*

Trick or Treat: A History of Halloween

Winner of the Bram Stoker Award® and the Halloween Book Festival Grand Prize

"Morton is an accomplished horror short story writer, and her ability to draw readers in quickly and keep them turning the pages shines through in her nonfiction as well. Lavishly illustrated, this solidly researched and concise work is fun to read and a great choice for readers who want to know why we seek out the scary each October." – Becky Spratford, *Library Journal*

"Like a candy bag full of historical nuggets and strange folklore, Lisa Morton's *Trick or Treat? A History of Halloween* is the perfect bible for all devoted disciples of the holiday." – Michael Dougherty, Writer & Director, *Trick 'r Treat*

"In a modern world, increasingly filled with pop culture fads and gimmicks, Lisa Morton reveals much of the underbelly history and unknown facts regarding the biggest pop culture event in history – Halloween. Her sheer delight and well-researched enthusiasm in tackling many of the unrecognized aspects of this monstrous topic makes one wonder what we don't know about everything else that should be as commonplace to our psyche as a bag of candy." – Del Howison, Bram Stoker Award-winning editor of *Dark Delicacies* and *Book of Lists: Horror*

"With *Trick or Treat* Lisa Morton gives us a charming, creepy, insightful and thoroughly fascinating history of Halloween. It's a delicious blend of cultural history and pop-culture savvy that is a true delight to read!" – Jonathan Maberry, *New York Times* best-selling author of *Flesh & Bone* and *Assassin's Code*

"This is an excellent survey of the Hallowe'en scene, informative and accessible, far more treat than trick." – Kim Newman, author of *Nightmare Movies* and *Anno Dracula*

"Simply the best book about Halloween I have ever read and if you are a fan of the holiday like I am, this is a must add to your library!" – Tim Janson, Mania.com

"From an authority on Hallowe'en lore comes all you need to know about this 'misunderstood' festival...Well-written and illustrated, informative and entertaining." – *Fortean Times*, October 2014

The Halloween Encyclopedia

"...Morton's research extends to Wiccan lore, Celtic observances, and Christian mythology...she writes enthusiastically about folk customs and is sensitive to the controversies surrounding horror literature, witchcraft, and demonism. Without undue pedantry, she explains the house-to-house souling pilgrimage, the incorporation of cabbages in Scottish holidays, the source of the boogeyman in bogs, and the lengthy training of Druid priests...this generously illustrated and indexed overview is a worthy addition to public and school libraries as well as the reference shelves of journalists and leaders of community events." - *Booklist Reference Books Bulletin* Volume 100, Number 14, March 15, 2004

"...Lisa Morton's tome is chock full of interesting facts...adroitly written and impressively researched, the encyclopedia draws on a myriad of works – folklore collections, Catholic and Irish histories, scholarly studies of paganism and witchcraft, newspaper accounts – to cover an impressive range of subjects..." - *Brutarian Quarterly* Number 42, Summer, 2004

"Lisa Morton has captured the 'spirit' of this 'hallowed' holiday in her new book. Herein, she's covered every angle (cultural, pop-cultural, historical, spiritual, and traditional 'harvest') of Halloween...Read this book to become an expert on the topic of Halloween!...This isn't just another stale piece of candy. Monster lovers like me, who love Halloween, will find this is one well worthwhile ." – Allen A. Debus, *Scary Monsters Magazine* Fall 2003

"...wonderful images of Halloween...Appendices also add an important and useful element...a well-researched and well-developed work. Not only covering the popular culture's impact on the current holiday, but also exploring how folk traditions from various cultures have woven together to become the holiday we celebrate today...a must have for public libraries."– Tim Daniels, *Emerald Reference Reviews* Vol. 18, No.2, March 2008

A Hallowe'en Anthology: Literary and Historical Writings Over the Centuries

Winner of the Bram Stoker Award® and nominated for the Black Quill Award

"Wikipedia is awesome, but we still need books...[collects] as complete an anthology as can be found of original mterial related to our favorite fest...for deeper understanding of the folklore, customs and literature related to October 31, this anthology is a must-have all year round." – Liisa Ladouceur, *Rue Morgue Magazine* Number 83, October 2008

"...Morton takes us on a fantastic journey through the evolution of Halloween. The book's twenty-seven entries are an exquisite, thoughtfully selected arrangement...*A Hallowe'en Anthology* is not simply for adults, but could easily be shared with children of any age, reigniting the tradition of storytelling so lacking in today's modern home...For anyone who enjoys Halloween, I highly recommend selecting this book as part of your holiday reading..." – Gabrielle Faust, FearZone.com, October 30th, 2008

"...presents a wealth of Halloween background and lore that includes astonishingly beautiful photo reproductions of Halloween artwork...This Halloween compendium is a magnificent achievement..." – J. L. Comeau, *Creature Feature Tomb of Horror*

The Cinema of Tsui Hark

"...a labor of love...provides a thorough look...Morton writes with great passion, providing a worthy analysis of the director's filmography that accurately relays the sense-heightening thrills of Tsui's best work...succeeds in offering a fine profile of a remarkable talent." – John Charles, *Video Watchdog* Magazine #88, October 2002

"If I were forced to make a list of my favorite Hong Kong movies, titles like *Iron Monkey, Time and Tide, Black Mask* and the *Once Upon a Time in China* series would be included. All these have in common the involvement of writer/director/producer Tsui Hark, one of the most creative filmmakers not only in his homeland, but all the world. Morton clearly has a love for her subject, which gives her book a sense of energy, but thankfully never treads into ass-kissing. It begins with an essay that serves as a nice overview to Hark and his wildly varied career. The majority of the book is taken up by analyses of each film, but the real meat is a lengthy Q&A with Hark himself. He seems like a smart guy (so one wonders why he said yes to Van Damme twice) and Morton takes a similar approach with her well-written book – a must for Hark and HK film fans." – *Hitch* Magazine #29, Spring 2002

"A must for Asian-Cinema buffs, Morton's tome offers a thorough, impassioned exploration of prolific producer/director/writer/actor Tsui (*Peking Opera Blues, Once Upon a Time in China*) Hark's major and minor films, along with a brief bio and running commentary by the man himself." – *VideoScope* Magazine #41, Winter 2002

"...Lisa Morton's book is a valuable introduction to the films of Tsui Hark and it is indispensable for any future studies." – Tony Williams, *Film Quarterly* Magazine, Vol. 56 No. 1, Fall 2002

Savage Detours: The Life and Work of Ann Savage

"...*Savage Detours* is not only a good look at the actress and her work, but also at the B-movie industry in the '40s and the life of the studio contract player. Briskly written, never dull or stodgy, it's an entertaining and informative read." – Michael Cornett, *Scarlet*, Autumn 2010, Issue #6

"*Savage Detours: The Life and Work of Ann Savage* by Lisa Morton and Kent Adamson is the book that belongs in the library of every film noir fan. It reveals the challenging life of a tough cookie who took her work very seriously, even though, for many years, she was the only one who did..." – Monica Sullivan, *Movie Magazine International*

"*Savage Detours* is a gem for fans of film noir, Ann Savage, the history of Hollywood B-films, and the film *Detour*. It's full off insights and inside information." – Matt Dukes Jordan, *Pulp Metal Magazine*

"I love this book...the biography section is exceptional. The writing throughout is honest but also warm and appreciative...the photos are simply mouthwatering...extraordinary work by the authors...I cannot rave enough. I'm in love with the idea of a book about the tremendous Ann Savage, one of my very favorites, but tickled that it's actually a wonderful, worthwhile book." – Laura Wagner, *Classic Images* November 2010, No. 425

Adventures in the Scream Trade

Also by Lisa Morton

Non-Fiction
The Halloween Encyclopedia
Ghosts: A Haunted History
The Cinema Of Tsui Hark
Trick or Treat: A History of Halloween
Savage Detours: The Life and Work of Ann Savage (with Kent Adamson)

Fiction
The Free Way
The Lucid Dreaming
The Samhanach
The Castle of Los Angeles
Wild Girls
Hell Manor
Summer's End
Smog
The Lower Animals
Netherworld
Monsters of L.A.
By Insanity of Reason (with John R. Little)
The Devil's Birthday
Malediction
Zombie Apocalypse: Washington Deceased

Graphic Novels
Witch Hunts: A Graphic History of the Burning Times (with Rocky Wood and Greg Chapman)

ADVENTURES IN THE SCREAM TRADE

Lisa Morton

WESTERN LEGENDS PUBLISHING
Los Angeles | Paris | London

Adventures In The Scream Trade
Copyright © 2016
Lisa Morton and *Western Legends Publishing*

Artwork: © 2013 James Powell
Used with permission.

The essay "How I Surprised Myself and Became a Halloween Expert" originally appeared at *Cloth's Chapel*, the blog of Benjamin Kane Ethridge, as a guest post on October 22, 2011.

Interior Design
By John Palisano

Western Legends Logo Created by D.T. Griffith

All rights reserved.

ISBN-13: 978-1523957057
ISBN-10: 1523957050

Western Legends Publishing
P.O. BOX 1226
Hollywood, California 90078

www.facebook.com/WesternLegendsPublishing

Dedication

This one's for Tom and Bari Burman, my other family, who've made so many of the good things in this book happen, and who made it possible to live through the bad.

Acknowledgments

Extra big thanks to my pal Michael Marano, who heard a lot of these stories in epic late-night phone calls and told me to write them down.

Table of Contents

My Norman Rock(un)well Childhood......17

Motherships and Flying Cows:
My Life as a Modelmaker......28

How I Was the Screenwriter of Alien II...
For About Three Days......40

Fear and Loathing in Jackson, Mississippi:
The Beast Within......46

Syngenors and Little Dead Girls:
More '80s Horror Movie Adventures......56

Lightning Strikes...almost......59

Meet the Hollowheads: Greatest Hits......68

Adventures in Dumbass – er, I Mean,
Dinosaur City......78

The Play's the Thing...
to Make You Crazy, I Mean......93

Agents: Bloodsucking Leeches from Hell,
or Bloodsucking Leeches from Heaven?......109

Living in Toontown......120

Why Weed and Filmmaking
Don't Go Together
Like Chocolate and Peanut Butter......129

Little Stories......134

Some Stories Behind Stories......139

Go East, Young Woman......151

Back in La-la Land......161

I Get "Tested"......171

How I Surprised Myself
and Became a Halloween Expert......180

Who You Gonna Call?......184

Calling Doctor Morton......190

Afterword......195

Bio......198

Adventures in the Scream Trade

Dad educating me in the true meaning of terror.

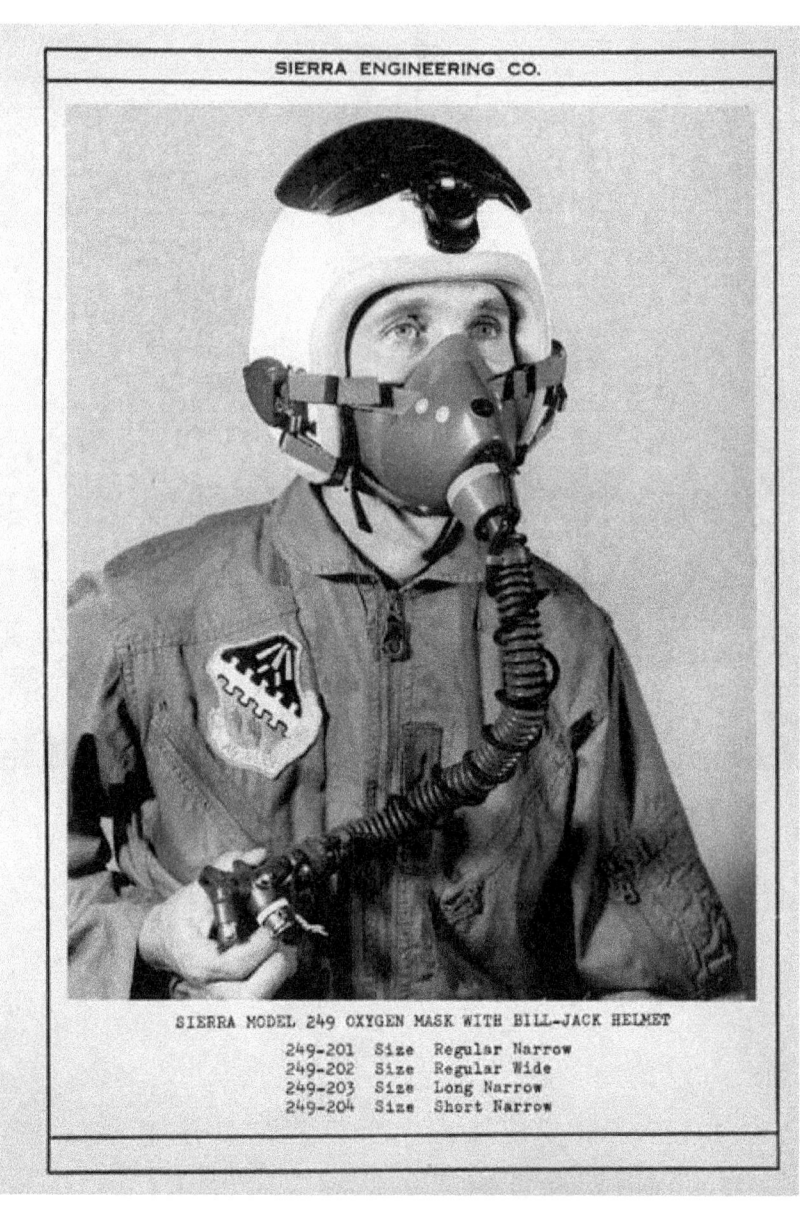

My genius pop demonstrating a helmet design.

My Norman Rock(un)well Childhood

I WAS BORN in a suburb of the San Gabriel Valley, half-an-hour east of Los Angeles (well, it was half-an-hour then; figure closer to an hour in 21st-century traffic), at a time when the Southern California smog was at its worst. Not that I'm using that as any sort of excuse for the behavior I will demonstrate in later pages, mind you, but it does partly explain my 20% reduced lung capacity and extreme dislike of exercise.

People are often surprised to hear me say that I'm a native Angeleno, because I've picked up a trace of accent from my folks. Both parents were Hoosiers (Indiana natives), and my dad in particular had a pronounced twang that I acquired. I also got the Mortons' primeval jaws (several of us have now undergone epic jaw surgeries), my dad's odd mix of logic and art, and a bent for theatricality (my paternal grandmother was an actress). From mom I got my love of reading, some freaky double joints (as a kid I'd watch *The Carol Burnett Show*, and whenever she'd pop her hip out of joint and leave the audience agog, I'd be thinking, Can't everyone do that?), and an unfortunate lack of assertiveness that I thankfully overcame early on. Lacking any siblings, I got it all.

Well, almost all. What I did not inherit from Dad was his hunting and fishing obsession. My dad, who I lost to cancer in 2015, loved to kill things. And eat them. Not, you know, like a zombie; he wasn't sitting around all the time drooling with uncontrollable bloodlust. But he lived for that moment when he was out in some godforsaken forest sighting down the rifle barrel at Bambi, or pulling Nemo up out of the water onto a boat (his last really happy event was a final fishing trip he and I took two months before he passed). I was practically middle-aged before I realized fully that this was not what he did for living. The man was a technological genius who had been involved with 36 patents (sadly few of which he owned, since he was always employed by someone else), including the liquid crystal, the modern computer motherboard, and the flight suits worn by the astronauts in the Mercury space program. Dad was always bringing me home stuff like rocket models and signed astronaut photos and so forth (and GOD, do I wish I had that stuff now). He was friends with Chuck Yeager and knew John Glenn.

But all I ever heard him talk about was deer hunting, or salmon fishing, or (worst of the worst, because it involves squatting in freezing mud for hours) duck hunting.

When I was little, we never took vacations like normal families. We never went to pretty foreign countries or to visit relatives or just to sightsee. No, we went to places like Idaho and Montana and (for the duck hunting, worst of the worst) Tule Lake. We didn't go in the summer, because hunting season didn't start until October; this meant that I usually got yanked out of school every fall, loaded into the truck, and driven nonstop for an entire day, at the end of which I was plunked down in the middle of bumfuck nowhere and waited in a cold, windblown camper until dad got his deer. Or duck. Or moose. Or pheasant. Or whatever it was.

Now granted, there were a few advantages to this. I'd have weird shit like venison jerky in my lunchbox every day, and for some inexplicable reason the other kids thought this was cool enough to trade me their Twinkies. I'd have actual animal hides to make into very authentic Halloween costumes. Mom would make me lots of hot chocolate while we huddled together in that camper that often shook from high winds.

But best of all was *Famous Monsters of Filmland*.

On every trip, we'd stop in the last civilized drugstore before plunging headlong into the Great and Freezing Wilderness, and I'd get to choose a book or magazine to take with me. My choice was invariably a magazine called *Famous Monsters of Filmland*. In case you're not familiar with this iconic emblem of 1960s culture, *Famous Monsters* (or simply *FM*) was largely a collection of black and white horror movie photos culled from the astonishing collection of its editor, Forrest J. Ackerman. Forry, as he was known to his legions of fans, provided simple stories liberally littered with silly puns to accompany the photos. Each issue had a beautiful color front cover, usually painted by an artist like Basil Gogos or Ron Cobb, and ads in the back for stuff like the "Frankenstein Speaks!" record and *Dick Smith's Do-It-Yourself Monster Makeup Guide* (both of which I still have).

So, while dad would disappear into the woods for days at a time, I'd be settled in with my *FM* (picture the magazine as already tattered when I bought it, probably having been thumbed through and returned to the rack of that drugstore in Oregon or Wyoming dozens of times) and Mom and hot chocolate. I'd leaf through those pages until the edges were shredded, absorbing every detail. By the time I was six, I was not only an avid reader, but could instantly tell you which Frankenstein movie Lon Chaney, Jr. had played the Monster in (*The Ghost of Frankenstein*, of course). It didn't even matter that I hadn't seen many of the films shown in the photos; my imagination ably filled in plots and characters. I loved cringing at certain horrible faces, feeling my tiny tummy turn at the goriest photos, or smiling in recognition at the monsters I did already know.

Back in those days, even though we had far fewer television stations, I swear they showed better movies. Universal endlessly syndicated all of their horror movies, the other studios had packaged all their classic horror and fantasy films, and even movies that have now virtually vanished could be seen almost any day of the month. Sometimes the channels would just show the same movie every day for a week, and I'd watch it every time (especially if it was *Journey to the Center of the Earth* or Karel Zeman's brilliant *The Adventures of Baron Munchausen*). I think I learned the basics of film construction watching those movies over and over.

So, here's a typical vacation for young Lisa: Dad's outside the door gutting a deer before roping it to the hood of the truck, and Lisa's trying to ignore this hideous act by gazing lovingly upon photos of monsters wreaking even bloodier carnage.

Yes, I grew up surrounded by blood. I helped clean fish, pound abalone, and carry dead fowl. Sometimes the blood was mine – on one trip, I tried to entertain myself by prospecting from the top of a cliff, lost my footing, and wound up with a backside still covered in scars as a result. I was obviously better off sticking to reading.

All of this is not to imply that my entire childhood was spent in gore. Back home, both my parents were more than happy to indulge my early love of horror and monsters. Mom and I would stay up late watching whatever horror movie came on; dad and I would build Aurora monster model kits together.

I also suspect both parents had a secret penchant for spooking me. Mom told me stories (which she now denies) of getting horrible worms from eating raw cookie dough. With Dad, I've got photographic proof, at least – a photo of me as a toddler, gasping and shrinking back as Dad, kneeling to meet my pint size, thrusts a toothy barracuda right into my shocked little face. I also have a vivid memory of Dad and Disneyland: We were visiting the "20,000 Leagues Under the Sea" exhibit, which used to exist in Tomorrowland and featured sets and scenes from the Disney film, and at one point there was a porthole that was slightly too tall for me to see through. Dad, grinning, picked me up and held me up to the porthole – which of course looked onto the giant squid, its dinner plate-sized eye staring back at me, its massive tentacles suspended in blue-green lighting that convincingly conveyed the illusion of being underwater. That thing both terrified and fascinated me, and became an integral part of my psyche afterward.

On another trip to Disneyland (who'd have thought that The Happiest Place on Earth could play so crucial a part in the making of a horror writer?), we encountered the Phantom of the Opera standing before the Main Street Cinema (and don't tell me that the Phantom was a Universal monster and would never have appeared at Disneyland and I'm obviously remembering it all wrong – he most certainly was there circa 1964, and I've got proof). Of course I loved the Phantom in the pages of *FM*, but being presented with him live and in color was pretty intense. Well, you know Mom and Dad had to have a photo of me with the Phantom, but I was apparently just too terrified to shoulder all the way up to him. I got within about ten feet.

Something else happened to me at six that I'm sure influenced much of my later life: I tripped out on a mistaken prescription. I'd had a bug of some sort for a while (I got everything as a kid), and Mom took me to the doctor, who prescribed antibiotics. What Mom didn't know was that the nice pill vial from the pharmacist held something that was most certainly not antibiotics, but some sort of hallucinogen (this was 1964 and LSD was still legal – I've wondered if that was what I got). Mom gave me the first two pills, and for most of a day I saw sweaters twisting into talking monkeys, and the car antenna (as Mom ran me back to the doctor, my eyes big as saucers) forming itself into Pinocchio. Oddly, these visions are among my strongest memories of childhood, and I'm always sort of amazed that I didn't see anything horrible. I've also never had any interest in drugs since; it's hard to top an acid trip at six, after all.

Being a monster-loving little girl already marked me as an instant weirdo (Weird-Ohs – another cool '60s thing! But I digress), but there was something that made me even weirder: My IQ. It would seem it was…ummm…rather extraordinary. I truthfully think I just had a spectacular aptitude for taking IQ tests (if I was as smart as they said, I'd be a millionaire now, right?). Whatever; by the time they'd studied the results of my first test, I was a marked target. I got tested at least once a year. I got pulled out of class and paraded to janitor's closets (yes, really) where I'd be given freakier and freakier tests. My parents would be called in for chats with principals…who weren't even the principals of my school, mind you. It seems that I basically outscored the tests' abilities to score. All they knew was that my IQ was somewhere above 190 and I had a photographic memory. They wanted me to go to special schools, which of course were invariably located… well, I don't know, in Wyoming or something. Maybe they taught deer hunting and nuclear physics.

I always said no. I liked my current schools. I was never particularly fond of the other kids, who frankly bored me, but I loved my teachers, several of whom taught me much of what I now know about writing.

I'm probably lucky I grew up when I did; if I was a kid now, I'd likely be bullied endlessly. But somehow – whether we just didn't have that back then, or I was so much of an outsider that I was left alone – I was ignored, and happily so.

Throughout my childhood, as I was tested and prodded and lectured by counselors, it was assumed that I'd eventually go into the sciences. I loved anthropology and archaeology, and I won a science fair in junior high with some kind of highfalutin' exhibit on the processes of evolution in homo sap. But then it all changed when I was 15.

When I saw *The Exorcist*.

If you needed any further proof that I have an amazing mom, this was it: She had not only let me read the novel when it was basically verboten among my age group, she also took my best friend and I to see the movie, back when "R-rated" was taken a lot more seriously. On an evening in March of 1974, we stood in a two-hour line, listening to people inside scream, and then watching the shocked survivors stagger from the theater as if they'd just witnessed a holocaust.

It's almost impossible to describe now, because no movie since has affected audiences like *The Exorcist* did. Don't tell me, "Well, there was *The Blair Witch Project* or *Paranormal Activity*", because I will laugh in your face and call you a sucker. *The Exorcist* absolutely and utterly terrified people, on some level so deep I'm not sure it's possible to do again. I sat in a theater with a thousand other moviegoers on that March night, and watched as people flinched, cringed, screamed, fled (in droves, after the head-turning), and fainted as the film progressed. Fully a fourth of the audience couldn't make it to the end; my friend, Susan, was a noticeable shade of green as we left the theater. During that spring, a hollow-eyed waitress or shaking bank teller meant they'd seen *The Exorcist*. *Time* Magazine wasn't kidding when they had a cover story describing the film's impact as a "frenzy".

That first viewing, however, was quite a different experience for me. It was the most revelatory two hours of my life.

I spent as much time watching the audience as the film (I went back to see the film ten more times during its first release, whenever I could get Mom to drop me off and buy me a ticket again). I was astonished by what that film did to an audience. I'd never realized that a work of art – a movie, for Christ's sakes – could have that kind of effect. I wanted to move people on that primal level…or at least try.

I walked into that theater wanting to be an anthropologist. I walked out wanting to be a writer.

It really was that simple. *The Exorcist* changed my life. Yes, I'd grown up on a diet of monster and horror films, but somehow it had never occurred to me that producing that sort of entertainment was something I wanted to do for a living. It took *The Exorcist* to wake me up.

Within a short time I was telling my school counselors that I wanted to study film and writing. This, needless to say, did not go over well when it came from the lips of the pet brainiac. "No, that's not what you want," they told me. "Your aptitude tests indicate the sciences."

And they had their way for a while. I was never allowed to take any of the few film courses offered at my high school. Creative writing was something reserved only for a few isolated hours during my English classes. I was already winning essay contests and had a short story published after a teacher (unbeknownst to me) submitted it to a creative writing magazine, but that didn't matter.

I took my SATs, and scored a scholarship to basically the college of my choice. I picked UCLA, for its film courses (yes, nowadays I would probably opt for USC, but back then UCLA sounded like the better choice for a would-be screenwriter). My counselors had lost the fight; my parents just kind of stepped back and let me have my determined way.

And so, out of dead animal blood and monster magazines and a gallon of onscreen pea soup and a tab of acid, a horror writer was finally born.

Me buried in the depths of V'Ger during *Star Trek: The Motion Picture*

Our large Ed Harris puppet from *The Abyss*, prior to his rapid descent.

Motherships and Flying Cows:
My Life as a Modelmaker

IT'S DIRTY CONFESSION TIME: I didn't finish college.

Sometime around my third year, I started to get bored and irritated. I turned out to not love college; at UCLA, film studies consisted of watching endless foreign films with titles like *W.R.: Mysteries of the Orgasm*. I found it all pretentious and stifling and more than a little silly. And no one seemed to be able to tell me exactly how long I had left; in high school, I'd taken and passed enough AP (Advanced Placement) courses that I'd theoretically knocked an entire year of college off, but – big surprise! – UCLA wouldn't accept those credits. Gee, kinda wish they'd told us that in high school, when money was tight and we'd had to scrimp and save to come up with the large fees they charged for those tests.

At some point I transferred to San Diego State – my mom and dad had divorced, and Mom was living in San Diego – hoping to find more practical hands-on training there. But near the end of my third year, when we were still making 8mm movies, I went to the head of the film department and asked when exactly we'd get to using real cameras and equipment, and start learning the real skills that would get us a job in the industry.

"Don't worry about it," this esteemed, white-haired dean of the film school told me, "none of you will ever get a job in the film industry anyway."

Well, here's what Mr. High and Mighty Dean didn't know: I'd already had offers to work in the industry. As a young film buff and genre fan, I'd attended dozens of science fiction conventions around the west coast already, and I'd made some interesting friends. One was a gentleman named Charles Lippincott, who in 1976 was telling me about a little movie he was working on called *Star Wars* that was coming out next year. Charlie and I would sit at conventions and talk about the movie and his job (he was in charge of marketing). At one point Charlie asked me if I'd like to interview for a position on the film, heading its official fan club. At 18, I found myself in an office in Hollywood, pretending to be a grown-up who knew something about marketing; eventually it came down to me and one other guy, but they did the smart thing and hired the guy who'd actually done tons of similar work. I was just grateful for the interview, and my first brush with film industry employment. Oh, and you probably know what happened to the little movie.

Another friend was named Bill George. Bill was an amazingly gifted modelmaker who'd been one year behind me in high school. Bill and his brother Bobby and our friend Kelly Turner (who went on to become a vice president at Virgin's gaming division and who sadly passed away at far too young an age) were all so smitten with the film-buff bug that we used to conduct late-night raids on the garbage bins of special effects houses. I knew about the effects company ILM through my *Star Wars* connections; this was when they were still located in a warehouse in Van Nuys. We used to hit their dumpster late at night, loading up the car with rolls of test footage and storyboard drawings. We learned a lot about the special effects biz courtesy of that trash.

One night we got caught. And it was great.

They were amazed that fans cared enough to hit the garbage bin. They invited us in and gave us a tour. They showed us how the camera worked; John Dykstra was head of ILM at the time, and had just invented the motion control camera. It was awesome.

They even let us keep the trash.

Bill used to display his own models at the conventions, and somewhere along the line he'd come to the attention of a man named Greg Jein. Greg is, very simply, the greatest miniatures artist in history. He's also a massive cinephile with a huge collection of memorabilia, and he used to haunt the conventions adding to his treasures. He's funny and soft-spoken and an all-round good guy, and he and Bill and I hit it off.

Sometime around 1979, he'd told us that if we ever wanted to work for a few days, he could always use extra help. Bill took him up on that offer almost immediately, and with his tremendous talent he fit right in (Bill, by the way, went on to win an Oscar for effects on *Innerspace*). My modelmaking experience was limited to those Aurora monster models I'd built with dad, but what the hell – I was willing to work my ass off and wanted to be in the film biz and figured I could learn.

So, as I walked out of the dean's office that fateful day, I knew exactly where I was going.

A few days later I was working as a modelmaker for the legendary Greg Jein on *Star Trek: The Motion Picture*. They were nearing the end of the show, and needed extra hands to meet deadlines. What started as a couple of days of work turned into a couple of long weekends.

It was exhausting and confusing and sometimes physically painful, and of course I loved every second of it.

We were working in a warehouse in the Marina del Rey area of Los Angeles. *Star Trek* was so big that nearly every warehouse on Mindanao Avenue had been taken over for the show. We worked in one dedicated almost solely to "V'Ger", the massive alien construction that served as the film's antagonist. Down the street was where they were filming the Enterprise and the matte paintings. Douglas Trumbull was in charge of the effects.

If you don't know the name Douglas Trumbull, then you need to brush up on your film history. Trumbull, as far as I'm concerned, is one of the real geniuses of cinematic history. He started with Kubrick's *2001: A Space Odyssey*, directed (and provided effects for) *Silent Running*, created the stunningly beautiful visuals for *Close Encounters of the Third Kind*, went on to do *Blade Runner*, and created a new camera and projection system called Showscan that should have revolutionized the industry, but somehow never caught on.

It didn't matter that I was nowhere near Trumbull most of the time, or even that I – who had been a total Trekkie geek as a kid – was working on the first *Star Trek* movie. What mattered was that I was 20 years old and I was working for two legends. It rocked.

I labored alongside a bunch of great guys: In addition to Bill, there was Nick Seldon, who has remained a lifelong friend, and Bob Short, a multi-talented guy who was always quick-witted and fun. And that was good, because we needed quick-witted and fun to get us through the frequent late nights and occasional all-nighters.

Greg and the others had enough (misplaced) faith in me to toss me headlong into the mix. I learned very quickly about special glues and plastics and how not to hold fiberglass, after turning my bare arms into bloody pulp just carrying a raw fiberglass panel for a few yards. I learned that the smell of two-part epoxy nearly made me sick, and that I wasn't a coffee drinker, and that the styrene glue I was splashing around so easily was probably eating away my liver. I learned how to use a Dremel Mototool and a Makita Drill, just like the boys. I spent hours and hours inside the massive shell of V'Ger, stringing fiber optic lights and adding tiny details that the camera would never see. Nick and I built the "hexagon bridge", a massive collection of tiny plaster blocks that we had to glue into very precise order to create an illusion of diminishing size.

Through it all, I had no illusions about my skills as a modelmaker. I knew these guys were being extraordinarily generous in letting me continue to work for them, and I tried to return the favor by joking and keeping spirits up and taking on the jobs no one else wanted and hanging out with them even when we weren't slaving away.

And it worked, because I was asked back to work on Greg and Trumbull's next project, *Close Encounters of the Third Kind: The Special Edition*.

But before that, there was a little business to be taken care of...

At the end of *Star Trek*, we were all given the chance to buy a crew jacket (and yes, those of us far down the ladder usually have to buy our own crew t-shirts and jackets; I think even later on, when I was the honest-to-God screenwriter, I still had to buy my own crew t-shirts). This was the disco era, remember, so the crew jackets were these canary yellow satin abominations with the film's logo on the back and our names stitched on the front. At the time I thought it was the most beautiful thing I'd ever seen (and yes, I do still have it, even though it's now even uglier and frayed and I wouldn't be caught dead wearing it).

So I got my jacket, put it on, and walked back to visit that college dean who'd told me I'd never get a job in the industry.

He just stared at me, dull-eyed, and I actually ended up feeling sorry for the man. I realized that because he'd never succeeded, he just assumed none of his students would, either; and most of the time he was right.

But damn, I still enjoyed that day.

By now, I was overdue for returning to school. My parents were horrified; my dad even went so far as to try to enroll me without my participation. But cripes, I already had my next movie job lined up. There was no way in hell I was going back to that useless, stupid college.

So I went on to *Close Encounters of the Third Kind: The Special Edition*.

I once again worked for Greg Jein, and since I came in almost from the start, this job went longer. Our crew built the interior of the Mothership that would provide the new climax for the film. Other crews were off building the "Cotopaxi", the ship found in the desert at one point, but we were making spaceship columns and hundreds of inch-tall aliens mounted to rods that could be wiggled to make them appear to move.

Now, here's something you need to know: Modelmakers pull a lot of all-nighters, not because they're slow, but because the directors and producers and production designers change their minds. A lot. And just because they've decided something should look completely different from the way it's just been built, that doesn't mean that the schedule gets extended. Those camera crews aren't about to be told that they can't start shooting tomorrow at eight a.m. as planned; so instead, the model crew stays up all night, redoing those damn miniatures, sometimes almost from scratch.

As a result, things sometimes get silly. Jokes get played. The jokes even work their ways into the models.

Bill George and his brother had a fake company they called Flying Cow Productions. For some reason that I've long since erased from my brain's databanks, they thought the phrase "flying cow" was the funniest thing on earth. As a result, I made tiny flying cows and stuck them onto the models where they wouldn't be seen. Or probably wouldn't be seen. At least I don't think anyone ever saw them, because they remained on the models throughout photography.

One tired day my Xacto blade slipped and I sprayed blood all over one of the columns of the Mothership. I, of course, immediately went for a towel, more concerned about the blood on the model than my own wellbeing. "No, don't!" Bill shouted, as he saw me reaching forward to wipe the blood away. I thought he knew something I didn't about the interaction between human blood and styrene. As it turned out, he really just wanted to permanently fix my blood to the model.

I can literally say I put my life's blood into that work.

Finally the show came to an end. The last night was our longest all-nighter yet; Spielberg had toured the model the night before, and ordered a number of last-minute changes that were fairly significant. We finished mere moments before the eight-o'-clock camera crew arrived.

However, I wasn't done. While the rest of the modelmakers staggered wearily home, I buddied up to the camera guys and asked if they'd let me watch some of the filming. I'd never actually seen a motion control camera in operation before, I wanted to see how it was done, and I figured this might be my last chance. They were kind enough to say yes, and I spent the next two hours in a dark, smoke-filled room watching the first filming of our Mothership model.

The whole thing was somewhat surreal. To give the illusion of atmospheric particles, the entire soundstage was filled with heavy smoke that settled into place and didn't move; those of us present had to stay in a small, enclosed booth. Because air conditioning would move the smoke around, it was turned off, and the powerful movie lights heated the space up quickly and uncomfortably. The camera sat on a track connected by cables to a computer, and it moved oh-so-slowly. A shot that would last only a few seconds on screen would take hours to film.

I left around 10 a.m., incredibly exhausted, and, frankly, more than a little depressed.

At that point I had no next job lined up. And I'd also realized that modelmaking was not what I wanted for a career. I'd learned more from a few precious weeks of working for Greg Jein than I had in three useless years of film school, but I felt like I'd reached a dead-end.

I wanted to be a screenwriter. Not a modelmaker.

So I took a job managing a bookstore. And still did small effects jobs on the side from time to time. It turned out I was quite good with still photography, and had a special talent for figuring out how to take great close-up photos of models (thank my dad's engineering genes for that). As a result, I got a few side photography jobs from my modelmaking buddies, and shot oddball things like stills that were used to storyboard the Clint Eastwood movie *Firefox*. My photos ended up appearing in all sorts of cool places, especially magazines like *American Cinematographer*, *Cinefex*, and *Fangoria*.

My one minor regret is that I didn't get onto *Blade Runner*, which is one of my favorite films. If I'd pushed, I probably could have...but by then I thought I was done with modelmaking.

As it turned out, modelmaking wasn't done with me. Nearly a decade later, when I'd finished my first movie as screenwriter and Associate Producer (*Life on the Edge*), and needed something to tide me over, I was offered a temp position on the modelmaking crew for *The Abyss*.

A temp position that ended lasting for the better part of a year.

I worked on *The Abyss* longer than any other movie, including the ones I wrote and helped produce. *The Abyss* went on and on and on. I had a wonderful, supportive boss named David Goldberg, and my immediate supervisor was a friend from *Life on the Edge*, Michael Stuart. There were a few other guys I already knew. I loved the whole crew, and working on the movie was an unexpected pleasure. For the first time, I actually demonstrated some talent for this modelmaking thing, and I was soon assigned to work with Henry Darnell making all the scale puppets. We made everything from tiny eight-inch tall divers who would appear clutching onto a submarine model to a large third-scale version of star Ed Harris, dressed in the white diving suit he wore in the film's climax. This beautiful, very lifelike fellow came to a heartbreaking end: To simulate Harris's descent into the abyss, our puppet was unceremoniously tossed from the side of a three-story building and filmed by a high-speed camera. Needless to say, weeks of detail work shattered on impact...but such is the life of a modelmaker.

Working on *The Abyss* took so long that our crew was actually moved during the production. We started in a big, drafty warehouse in Burbank (this place was often so cold in the mornings that I took to wearing fingerless mittens), and eventually moved to Simi Valley, where the DreamQuest effects facility was located. At the time, DreamQuest was on the cutting edge of the industry, and it was particularly exciting to be at their large (and heated) facility.

Now that we were closer to the action, so to speak, James Cameron began to appear more frequently. I liked him instantly; he was a perfectionist, and I've always been able to identify with perfectionists (gee, wonder why). He'd come from a modelmaking background, and maybe that meant he gave us a little extra leeway. One day he bought our model crew lunch, and we had a great time hanging with him in a big empty boardroom, chowing down like we were all old buddies. He was tough, and sometimes we had to do work over in ways that mystified us (I especially recall spending an entire day creating ripples of sand on a miniature of the ocean floor). But when he liked something and gave it his magic "PFD" (for Pretty Fucking Decent), you felt like you'd earned it.

Being part of the model crew gave me access to the entire facility, and during breaks or after my work day, I roamed the joint, befriending everyone from laser effects experts to editors. I soon sussed out that something pretty special was going on with *The Abyss*, something involving the then-newborn art of computer graphics. One day my editing buddies waved me into their cutting room and shut the door.

"You've gotta see this," they told me breathily.

They then ran a ten-minute chunk for me that they'd just finished cutting. It wasn't a sequence that involved any of the models I'd worked on for months, but rather centered on the computer effects. It was the scene where the alien pseudopod invades Deep Core and takes on the faces of the actors.

It was mind-blowing. It was the future.

And it was the obvious end of modelmaking.

We all sensed it as the film wound down. Some of my friends were already segueing into art direction. Others moved into propmaking. But the writing was on the wall for modelmaking.

Fortunately for me, I got my next screenwriting gig just as *The Abyss* was ending, and it turned out to be a fantasy film that I was able to bring some of my modelmaking friends onto. But I knew *The Abyss* would be my grand finale as a modelmaker.

Sadly I didn't receive credit on the film – there were so many modelmakers employed on *The Abyss* that they basically held a lottery to determine who among the grunts would get credit, and I lost out – but the studio kindly acknowledged those of us who were cut from the credits in a special trade ad, and I got invited to the crew screening and was given all kinds of nice stuff. And the crew jacket for *The Abyss* rocked: It was a heavy, all-black letterman-style jacket featuring patches from the film and my name sewn inside. It's actually still an attractive, useful jacket, probably the warmest item of clothing I own (hey, I live in Southern California).

I've also heard that I show up on one of the many documentaries produced about the film, but I've never watched them. Frankly, it would be kind of anti-climactic.

After all, I lived it. Or, as one of the crew t-shirts read – "Life's Abyss and Then You Dive".

"ALIEN II- RETURN"

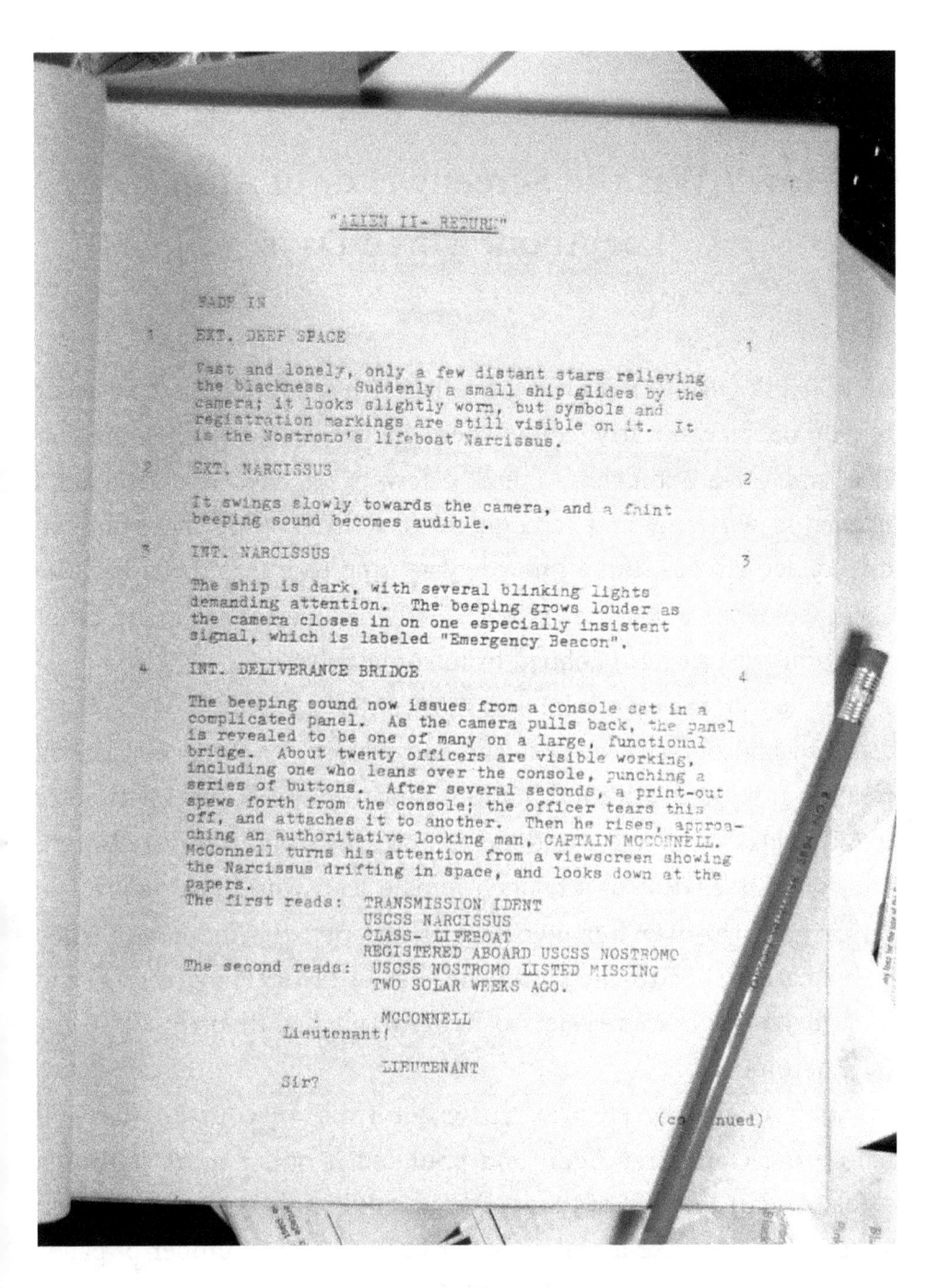

FADE IN

1   EXT. DEEP SPACE

Vast and lonely, only a few distant stars relieving the blackness. Suddenly a small ship glides by the camera; it looks slightly worn, but symbols and registration markings are still visible on it. It is the Nostromo's lifeboat Narcissus.

2   EXT. NARCISSUS

It swings slowly towards the camera, and a faint beeping sound becomes audible.

3   INT. NARCISSUS

The ship is dark, with several blinking lights demanding attention. The beeping grows louder as the camera closes in on one especially insistent signal, which is labeled "Emergency Beacon".

4   INT. DELIVERANCE BRIDGE

The beeping sound now issues from a console set in a complicated panel. As the camera pulls back, the panel is revealed to be one of many on a large, functional bridge. About twenty officers are visible working, including one who leans over the console, punching a series of buttons. After several seconds, a print-out spews forth from the console; the officer tears this off, and attaches it to another. Then he rises, approaching an authoritative looking man, CAPTAIN MCCONNELL. McConnell turns his attention from a viewscreen showing the Narcissus drifting in space, and looks down at the papers.
The first reads: TRANSMISSION IDENT
                   USCSS NARCISSUS
                   CLASS- LIFEBOAT
                   REGISTERED ABOARD USCSS NOSTROMO
The second reads: USCSS NOSTROMO LISTED MISSING
                   TWO SOLAR WEEKS AGO.

                MCCONNELL
        Lieutenant!

                LIEUTENANT
        Sir?

(continued)

Page one of *Alien II: Return*

How I Was the Screenwriter of *Alien II*... For About Three Days

AFTER I'D DROPPED OUT of college (that sounds so deliciously rebellious, doesn't it?), somewhere in between working on *Star Trek* and *Close Encounters*, I had a few extra days and decided I needed to write my first screenplay. I'd written some short films in my college classes, but I knew it was time to find out if I had the chops to write a feature. I proceeded to do what so many other first-time writers do: I cobbed from somebody else.

And wrote my own sequel to *Alien*.

Alien had opened towards the end of May 1979, so it was still fresh in my mind. Its combination of horror and science fiction, of working class characters and elegant creature, had captivated me... and, of course, best of all was a female lead who didn't squeal in terror and trip over her own feet as she fled the monster. Ripley immediately shot to the top of my list of favorite characters, and for a beginner it was easier to write about her than to create my own heroine.

So I set up my electric typewriter (this, of course, was well before the Computer Age), and pounded it out. I think it took a week. And at the end of that week, lo and behold – I had a finished script. It looked like a real script, it had the right number of pages and was properly formatted, and it had my name on the title page.

I took it with me when I went back to work on *Close Encounters*; I knew some of the other guys on the modelmaking crew were also interested in writing, so I passed it around. Everyone seemed to really like it.

But the most gratifying early response came from someone who couldn't have read more than half-a-page. One day I was sent from our little modelmaking conclave down to the main offices at the end of the block to get something. For some reason I had the script with me, and when I had to wait, I sat down and started re-reading a few pages. I suddenly realized that someone was standing behind me, reading over my shoulder. I looked up at my reader.

"What's that?" he asked.

"Oh…it's a sequel to *Alien*."

"Did you write it?"

I managed a weak nod.

He grinned and turned to walk off, but not before throwing back very loudly, causing a few heads to turn, "It's good! You should get it in!"

That man was Douglas Trumbull.

Fast-forward to a year or so later. I was now managing a bookstore in Century City, taking the occasional effects job on the side, and trying to work on original screenplays. One day a handsome young fellow approached me at the store; one of the other employees had told him I was a modelmaker, and he was a big special effects fan. His name was Paul Clemens. He said he was an actor.

Now, if you spend any amount of time in L.A., probably a third of the people you meet will tell you they're an actor (another third will say they're producers, and of course all of them are working on screenplays, because nobody ever actually sets out to be just a screenwriter). Even at 21, my bullshit meter was already in place, and I had no reason to believe this guy more than anyone else.

Except he wasn't just an actor. He was Hollywood Royalty.

On our second date, Paul revealed to me that his mother was the actress Eleanor Parker. Nowadays, most people would know her (if at all) as the Baroness in *The Sound of Music*. But in the '40s and '50s, Eleanor Parker was not only one of the most beautiful women in show biz, she was also known as "the actress's actress". She'd been nominated for three Academy Awards, and had worked with virtually every major star in Hollywood (including my personal favorite, Errol Flynn, who she told me had called her "Grandma" due to her very proper behavior). Paul's father had been a preeminent painter whose portraits hung in the White House. He'd grown up in a mansion in Beverly Hills, surrounded by servants and step-siblings. His mother had returned from *The Sound of Music*, and presented Paul with a duplicate set of the adorable puppets used in the film. Paul had promptly beheaded them and buried the little wooden bodies in the garden.

There was a reason we were together.

And Paul really was an actor. In 1978, he'd starred in an acclaimed television movie called *A Death in Canaan*, which was based on the true story of a teenaged boy who was essentially brainwashed by police into confessing to the murder of his mother. *A Death in Canaan* had co-starred fine actors like Kenneth McMillan, Tom Atkins, and Stefanie Powers, and had been directed by one of those artful British directors I'd studied in college, Tony Richardson. Not long after, Paul gave another fine performance in a dramatic feature film, *Promises in the Dark*, in which he played the sympathetic boyfriend of a teenage girl dying of cancer.

One night, while strolling the trendy college area of Westwood, two young men hesitantly approached Paul, confirmed his identity, and proceeded to wax rhapsodic over him for the next twenty minutes. They were actors, they said. The younger one said that Paul's performance in *A Death in Canaan* was what had inspired him to pursue acting. He'd just finished shooting his first feature film.

That film was *Taps*. The young man's name was Sean Penn. The older man was his brother, Chris Penn.

Over the next few years, we somehow ran into Sean frequently. Once, he and his date, the actress Elizabeth McGovern, spotted us as they were leaving a theater, and we all spent some time chatting. Elizabeth asked me if I was an actress. I was simultaneously flattered that she thought I might be, and amused by the notion.

(Years later, I had a final Sean Penn spotting, when I stumbled across a couple arguing very loudly about exactly which one of them had locked the keys in the car. The couple was Sean and his at-the-time wife Madonna. I guessed – correctly! – that that marriage was destined to crumble.)

Paul knew a lot of interesting people. He was close to both Ray Bradbury and Forrest J. Ackerman. We went to parties at Forry's amazing house, the Ackermansion, and Forry even ran an article about me in the final *FM* he edited (talk about coming full circle – I actually got to appear in the magazine that had inspired me as a child). Ray took us to the set of *Something Wicked This Way Comes*, where I slyly snapped photos aplenty. At one point during the day, while Ray and Paul were off doing something else, I found myself chatting away amiably with Pam Grier, who was strikingly beautiful and very smart and committed to her role as the Dust Witch. Sadly, it wasn't until years later that I got to know Grier's work in the classic blaxpoitation movies, because I would have loved to have chatted with her about *Coffy* and *Foxy Brown*…but we had a lovely conversation nonetheless.

One day Paul told me that he'd met a woman named Linda who was a huge fan of his work, and she and her husband, a film producer, had invited us out to dinner. We accepted, and I soon found out that Linda's last name was Shusett. Her husband was named Ron.

Ron Shusett was indeed a real film producer. In fact, he had produced *Alien*.

We arrived at their home, and were introduced to a semi-conscious man on their couch who apparently lived there. That was my introduction to Dan O'Bannon, the gifted writer/filmmaker who had written the first draft of *Alien*'s screenplay (he and Ron had created the basic story together). Dan was suffering from some mysterious ailment at the time, and it wasn't until years later, when we had a chance meeting after some film screening or other, that I got to chat with a healthy, lively O'Bannon (at the time, he was planning *Return of the Living Dead* and was energized by it).

The Shusetts were lovely people, and finally I worked up the nerve to mention that I'd written my own sequel to *Alien*. I'm sure Ron was just being polite when he said he'd like to read it. But here's the astonishing thing: He really did read it.

And loved it.

Well, okay…so maybe "loved" is too strong a word. But he thought it was really, really good. So did Dan. Suddenly the dinners with Paul and Linda and Ron and I turned into lunch with just Ron and I, as we began to seriously discuss the script. He pointed out a couple of missteps. He said he and Dan would like to work on it.

There was just one little hitch (and you'll see that this is going to be possibly the predominant theme of my life from here on out): Shusett was only one of the producers on *Alien*. After the first film had become a smash, the producers had all started wrangling over exactly who owned the rights to do the sequel. It went to court. It got ugly.

Of course you already know the outcome, because you've all seen *Aliens*, the 1986 sequel written and directed by James Cameron. When the dust finally settled, Ron was out.

And so, of course, was my *Alien II*.

I hope you can understand when I tell you that it was, truthfully, hard for me to watch *Aliens*. I've mellowed over the years, and I can enjoy it on its own terms now. But here's what still bugs me about it: At the most basic level, it's exactly the same story as the first film. Here's the breakdown: Ripley, an android, and a crew of supporting meals – er, I mean, players – are sent by an evil corporation to a distant planet, where they confront nasty aliens. As those around her are picked off one by one, Ripley uses her courage and determination to survive, while also protecting a small sidekick. In the climax, as the area around her counts down to self-destruction, she battles the alien to protect her diminutive charge.

That was undoubtedly the smartest, safest way to do an *Alien* sequel. Cameron's film made a kazillion dollars.

Mine wouldn't have. Because it was strange and complex and kind of nihilistic. The central concept was that the evil corporation had sought out the aliens as superweapons, but after Ripley defeated one, their attention turned to her. After being held captive by them for weeks and subjected to freaky tortures and tests, she finally escapes and realizes she only has one shot: She needs to release the aliens on the corporation.

Alien II: Return is now over 30 years old, and has spent most of those years on a shelf gathering dust. It worked as both my affirmation that yes, indeed, I could write screenplays, and as my introduction to the ups and downs of Hollywood. One of these days I might just have to type it into this computer and release it into the wilds. It would be fun to see where it lands.

But in the meantime...there are other movies to talk about.

Halloween 1982: Me as Ripley dating the Beast Within

Fear and Loathing in Jackson, Mississippi: The Beast Within

I HOPE NO ONE came to these essays expecting energizing tales of overnight success. Or even over-YEAR success. There are a lot of "close but no cigar" anecdotes here, which explains why I remain perennially impoverished.

Paul Clemens, though, may be the King of Second Choices. When I was dating him in 1980, casting was underway for the film version of Judith Guest's novel *Ordinary People*. Paul had some sort of connection with the author, had read the book, and desperately wanted to play the teenage son, Conrad. Apparently Guest wanted him as well. Paul went through the usual audition process, and finally was one of two actors considered for the role.

There was just one teeny tiny thing (there always is): The film's director, Robert Redford, wanted a Conrad who looked gaunt. Paul had inherited his mother's glorious, wide cheekbones, and had also developed a junk food addiction; there was almost no way he was ever going to appear truly gaunt. However, they actually gave him two weeks to try. And at the end of the two weeks, he came back to the *Ordinary People* offices…and they promptly cast Timothy Hutton in the part.

He, of course, went on to win the Oscar for his performance.

Paul had also tied for the role of son Ben in *The Great Santini* with Robert Duvall. In the end, they decided they wanted someone more obviously athletic, and cast Michael O'Keefe.

O'Keefe was nominated for the Oscar. He lost to Timothy Hutton.

Paul lost to both of them.

However, he was about to land a role that, if hardly up to the critical standards of those two (hahahahaha!), was nonetheless ideally suited to a monster-loving boy: He would play the lead role of a cursed, monsterrific boy in a horror movie called *The Beast Within*.

On the surface, *The Beast Within* looked like gold. It was being made by a major studio (MGM) with a decent budget, it was based on a solid book (by Edward Levy), it was produced by Harvey Bernhard, who'd scored a megahit with *The Omen*, and it would be directed by a young Australian named Philippe Mora, whose previous feature film, *Mad Dog Morgan*, had received fantastic reviews.

However, if you're one of the 20 or 30 people who actually saw *The Beast Within* without benefit of alcohol or other addictive substances, then you know it wasn't gold. It wasn't even silver. Lead might be closer, as in…lead balloon.

It started well, though: Philippe Mora was an eccentric and fascinating man, with a constant twinkle in his eye and a gorgeous wife named Pamela. Philippe was very knowledgeable about film history and threw fabulous Hollywood parties. At one, I'd been amiably chatting with a nice British gentleman for several minutes before a stunning blonde woman joined him, and he introduced me to his wife – Theresa Russell. I abruptly realized he was Nicolas Roeg, one of my favorite directors. I'm sure I just stopped and gaped in disbelief for a few seconds and probably spluttered something about *Walkabout*, his 1971 film that's one of my favorites.

And then, of course, there was the make-up effects wizard hired for the film.

Anyone familiar with the history of special make-up effects knows the name Tom Burman. Tom had worked with John Chambers on the original *Planet of the Apes*, went on to perfect the use of bladder effects on movies like *The Manitou*, created the aliens for *Close Encounters of the Third Kind*, and even pulled off an astonishing dog make-up in the 1978 version of *Invasion of the Body Snatchers*. This guy was a legend...and he was going to be transforming my boyfriend into a murderous, malformed were-creature.

The day came when Paul had to head to Tom's studio in the San Fernando Valley to have a head cast and full body cast taken (the beast suit would be designed to fit him snugly). Paul didn't drive, and I of course wasn't about to give up an opportunity to meet Tom Motherfucking Burman, so we got in my Toyota and headed north. The studio was tucked away, quite innocently, in an industrial area in Van Nuys.

Here's where I get a little bit metaphysical on you all. We've all had that experience where we meet someone and feel that inexplicable instant connection, right? Like you just discovered a twin brother or sister you'd never known you had.

I had that with Tom. It didn't matter that he was nearly twenty years older than me, or that we were separated by gender, talent, years of experience in the industry, and money. We just connected instantly. If you'd told me fifteen minutes after meeting Tom that he would become an important fixture in the rest of my life, I would have told you simply, "Yes, I know."

After that first visit, Paul and I started hanging around the Burman Studio, watching as Tom and his crew created the many effects that would be needed for *The Beast Within*, everything from severed heads and body parts to midway transformation appliances (these are the foam pieces that are glued directly to an actor's face) to two complete Beast suits (one for Paul, one for a stunt double). Tom started teaching me sculpting, and weirdly enough I was pretty good at it. He patiently showed me how to work in the various clays, how to use specific tools and texture pads, and how to create wrinkles and folds of skin. Because I'm patient and steady, he wanted to teach me the laborious (but lucrative) art of hair-punching, but – as with modelmaking – I knew I wasn't cut out to do this for a living. We also talked a lot about writing, and soon started writing scripts together.

Finally *The Beast Within* was ready to start principal photography, and the entire crew moved to Jackson, Mississippi, where the film would be shot on location. I'd examined the shooting schedule, and picked the two weeks that involved most of the effects to visit. In the story, Michael's slow and bizarre transformation has landed him in a hospital, and those scenes were being shot in a real live mental institution.

So I flew to Mississippi, and soon found myself on the set at the institution. A documentary about this place would have been far creepier than *The Beast Within*. The facility still had a wooden sign out front that read "Lunatic Asylum", and it was obviously very old. Huge parts of it were no longer used; on the third floor that had been occupied by *The Beast Within* crew, there was only one functioning area – a beauty shop for female inmates. The most disturbing thing there was the basement: It had long ago been abandoned and was used only to store decaying old equipment (think cabinets with neck holes), the floor was covered in about two inches of slimy water, and someone had spray-painted smiley faces on the walls. Some of the actors told me that the facility's director had taken them to see the resident cannibal, all the while telling them excitedly about the time he escaped and partially ate a nurse. I never got to see the cannibal, but that same director did tell me all about hydrocephalic babies. He was a card, I tell ya.

The cast and crew were extraordinarily gracious to me, and I spent much of my time hanging out with Tom and the make-up effects guys. They'd taken over a large empty room near the main shooting area, where they kept all the various body parts, monster suits, and make-up pieces. One day a group of us were clowning around in that room, and two of the guys were tossing the fake severed head of actor Don Gordon like a ball. We all suddenly looked up, and saw a string of female patients gawking at us in incomprehension; no one had realized until then that the make-up room was located on the way to the beauty shop. *The Beast Within* probably seriously set back some of the patients' therapy.

The film's big make-up scene was a transformation; Michael, bedridden in a hospital, suddenly begins to transform into the beast before his terrified parents' eyes. This was going to be a piece de resistance for Tom, involving various stages with lots of make-up changes to Paul; for the final shots, Paul would be replaced by an articulated dummy that had sophisticated cable controls and was quite startling.

The transformation took the better part of two days to film. On the second day, as the dummy was brought in, Tom asked me if I'd like to help puppeteer. I of course was completely thrilled with this idea, and I ended up being assigned the operation of the puppet's long, bloated tongue. As the cameras rolled, Philippe would shout directions – "Lis, wiggle the tongue more!" Philippe, in fact, went absolutely apeshit with that dummy; he kept shooting way past what it had really been designed to do. He had the crew inflate the bladders in the head to the point where the whole thing looked like some absurd balloon about to pop...and then he kept it all in the film.

Several nights later, we were in a freezing cold southern forest at three in the morning (this was February, so it was practically still winter), as Paul, now encased in the full Beast suit, chased his cinematic girlfriend through the woods until he caught up to her and raped her, impregnating the poor girl the same way Michael's mother had been impregnated 17 years earlier. Paul was not exactly happy with having to do this; he spent much of the night apologizing to the stunt double they'd hired to sprawl naked below the Beast. Philippe, on the other hand, seemed to be having the time of his life. I stood behind the camera, shivering and watching my beau commit faux rape, and at the end of the take Philippe turned to me excitedly. "Well, Lis – was that effective?"

I assured him it was.

(Later on, as they went through the dubbing in post-production, Paul had to stand before a microphone while watching that footage and pretend to grunt and groan ala the Beast. At the end of that take, Philippe asked me the same question again.)

The Beast Within had an outstanding cast of supporting actors, and it was fabulous to spend some time with Ronny Cox, Bibi Besch, R. G. Armstrong, Logan Ramsey (who I'd work with again on *Life on the Edge*), Don Gordon, Meschach Taylor (who would later become a television star, thanks to *Designing Women*) and especially L. Q. Jones, because I very much admired a film he'd directed in the 1970s called *A Boy and His Dog* (based on Harlan Ellison's story). He was surprised that anyone had even seen the film, let alone liked it, but he seemed oddly reticent to talk much about it.

After shooting wrapped on *The Beast Within*, they moved into post-production, and there was still one big highlight waiting for me there. I'm a lifelong fan of movie soundtracks, and I was absolutely ecstatic when I found out Les Baxter would be scoring the film. I not only grew up hearing Les's exotic jazz, but I adored his scores for movies like *The Dunwich Horror* and Roger Corman's *House of Usher*. I'd always wanted to see a scoring session, and the producers were kind enough to allow Paul and me to observe on *The Beast Within*. The session took place at a recording studio in Burbank, and used a surprisingly large orchestra (I think it was 30 members). Scoring sessions are always entertaining to watch; I've been to several since, and I still love them. The musicians are all so highly trained that they rarely need even one rehearsal. They sit with their backs to a large screen, while the conductor faces the screen; the conductor watches as the film is projected, so he can keep the music in time to the scene. Usually the musicians have no idea what they're playing to. Les had written a superb cue to accompany the transformation, full of shivery strings and a slow, ominous build, and the orchestra played it perfectly the first time through. Afterwards, as the musicians all sort of said, "What the hell was that we just played?!", they ran the scene again, so they could watch. They all sort of stared in disbelief, and of course Philippe and the producers were delighted.

Unfortunately, audiences didn't take to *The Beast Within* quite like those studio players did. It was a strange hybrid in many respects – stuck somewhere between slasher and monster movie, between horror and black humor. Audiences burst into laughter at inappropriate moments; one of the film's biggest laugh-getters is Bibi Besch's line, "Can he travel?", delivered after seeing her son starting to monsterize in that hospital bed and thinking he just needs better medical care (Philippe once told me that line was intended to be funny, but I remain unconvinced). The film soon vanished from theaters, and is now little more than a barely-remembered oddity.

But it sure was fun while it lasted.

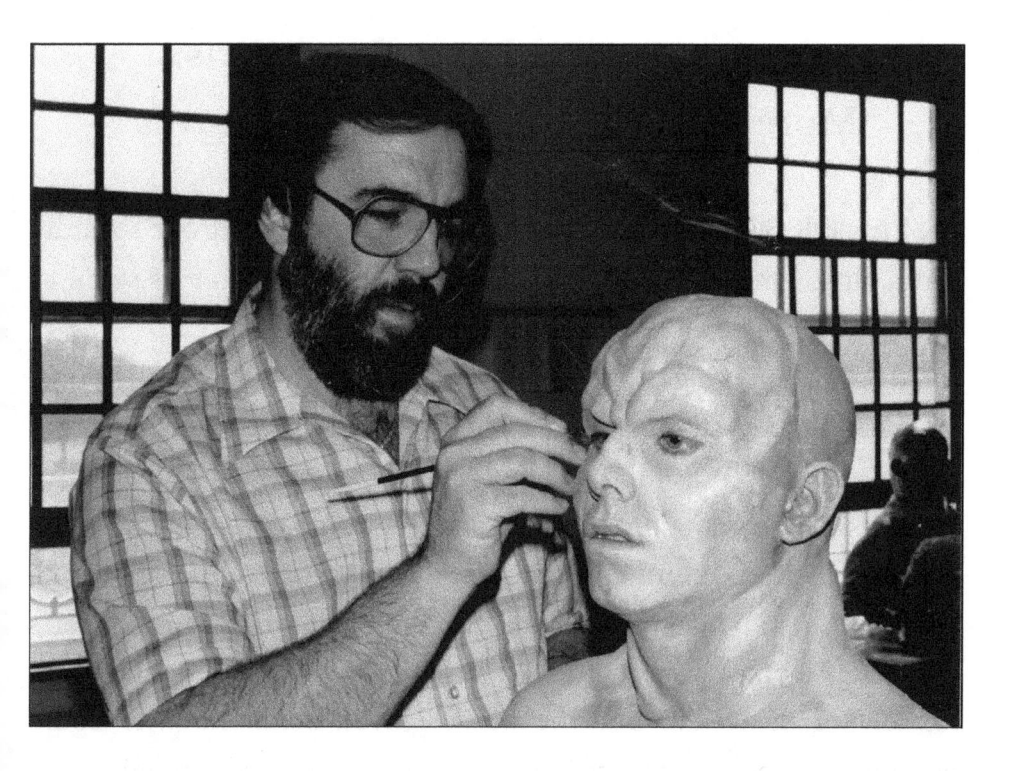

Tom Burman making up Paul Clemens for transformation midpoint in *The Beast Within*

Syngenors and Little Dead Girls: More '80s Horror Movie Adventures

A YEAR OR SO after *The Beast Within*, Paul and I went our separate ways, although we remained friendly and I would later use him as a stage actor in several productions.

I'd left managing a Waldenbooks behind when the Regional Manager held a seminar and told all of his store managers that there should be no difference between selling a book and a bar of soap (that line remains possibly the single most repugnant thing anyone's ever said in my presence). I had then taken up the life of a secretary in a small office loosely connected to the Producer's Guild. This office was incredibly slow and rarely had actual work for any of us to do, but the bosses loved someone who could nonetheless look busy, so I spent eight hours a day banging out scripts on my IBM Selectric typewriter. I like to say that was the first time I was paid to write.

On weekends, I'd still get calls from friends to come and help out on some set or other. My pal Bob Short, who I'd known from my *Star Trek* modelmaking days, had moved away from modelmaking and more into propmaking and make-up effects, and he liked having his work covered in photographs. He'd call me up and say, "Hey, I'm working on this movie called *Killbots* down at the Corman Studios…wanna come down and take some pictures?" So I'd show up with my trusty Canon A-1, thinking I was just going to shoot some particular stuff for Bob, and soon finding out that the production had no regular still photographer, so I ended up doing the official cast and crew photo and God knows what else (the movie was eventually released under the title *Chopping Mall*; I've never seen it, but assume it's horrid).

Another time, Bob was the head make-up guy on a movie he'd helped write, a sort of *Alien* variation called *Scared to Death*. On the day I was there, they were shooting a scene in a sewer tunnel where the hero would discover the drained and cocooned victims of the "Syngenor" (from Synthetic Genetic Organism…and I don't know why I still remember that). I started off taking photos, was soon helping Bob with some of the effects, and ended by playing one of the victims. Just another day on a B-movie set, in other words.

Far and away the best of the '80s horror movies I worked on was *One Dark Night*. I actually spent quite some time on this one, in between the bookstore and the office job, working for Tom as part of a medium-sized make-up crew. The film, written and directed by a talented young guy named Tom McLoughlin, centered on a telekinetic psychic who uses his powers to disinter corpses from a mausoleum and fly them around, chasing some terrified teens. We had to create dozens of corpses for the film, in various states of decay, and Tom wanted to make the corpses memorable, so we were each assigned particular corpses and instructed to try to make them individualistic. I had a little girl who had drowned, and I pored over actual photos of drowning victims, trying to make her both realistic and pathetic. Our bible on this film was a book called *Color Atlas of Forensic Pathology*, which was basically a collection of detailed color photos of people who had died in various ways. The book, of course, would have most folks putting their heads between their knees to recover, but by studying it for clinical details you would soon become completely detached from the gore on display. One afternoon I was examining it during a lunch break, thinking nothing of eating my sandwich over this thing, when some innocent visitor to the Burman Studio happened to ask what I was reading and glanced over. I'll bet they wondered what I had in the sandwich.

Anyway, I got to carry my little girl all the way from design to sculpting to casting to painting to dressing and even accessorizing (she still clutched a doll), and I was very pleased with how she turned out (I've even had people tell me it was their favorite corpse from the movie!).

One Dark Night is now chiefly remembered as marking the debut of Meg Tilly, but it also had another first: It was the first (and only) time I received on-screen credit for any of my effects work.

Lightning Strikes...almost

Paul Clemens posing before the honest-to-gawd real
"Lunatic Asylum" sign in Jackson

DURING MY FIRST DECADE as a screenwriter, I had lots of things optioned (for no money or next to no money), and I gathered lots of good comments (I even have a letter from Ray Bradbury about one of my scripts, and believe me – he was far too kind to it). I got used to promises and learned the hard lesson about taking everything you hear in Hollywood with a boulder-sized grain of salt.

But one script gathered some real steam, and threatened to turn into an honest-to-God movie.

Lightning Strikes was a big science fiction action thriller that was really my feminist response to *The Road Warrior*, a movie I'd loved. What if, I'd thought more than once after seeing the film, Mad Max was Mad Maxine? So I wrote this huge, insanely expensive script about a lone female warrior in a desolate future who travels around in an armored hovertank and runs into trouble when she finds what seems to be a functioning city. I'd thought through the notion of a female warrior at length, and tried to make sure that she didn't come off as merely a hero with breasts. I made her fast and wiry, so she could crawl in and out of places that muscled men couldn't, I made her smart and cunning, and I even took the risk of having compassion be both her greatest strength and biggest weakness. I gave her a hunky guy as a love interest (the leader of the city), and friends to protect. When she found out the secret of the city's wealth (institutionalized cannibalism), she led a revolt.

Lightning Strikes got passed around among my friends – a lot. It ended up in the hands of people I didn't know. People all loved it. It was optioned several times.

Finally a guy named Jack Teetor optioned it. Jack was a terrific fellow; he'd been a studio accountant who wanted to move into producing, and he thought *Lightning Strikes* could take him there. After he optioned the script, he started looking for a director.

The first director attached to *Lightning Strikes* was a woman named Barbara Peeters. Barbara had cut her directorial teeth for Roger Corman, making the cult favorite *Humanoids from the Deep*. Since that movie, she'd done lots of television, but was aching to get back into feature films. She had lots of fantastic ideas for

Lightning Strikes, and she soon brought two interesting actors into the project.

Ann Turkel was a strikingly beautiful Amazon who was chiefly known as Richard Harris's wife. She'd starred in *Humanoids* for Barbara, and she fell in love with *Lightning Strikes*. I truthfully thought she was too big for the role (so much for my notion of the heroine using her smaller size to escape in one crucial chase scene), but the camera loved her and she could probably give a solid performance.

If I had any reservations about Ann, there were absolutely none about the second actor brought onboard, considering that he was (astonishingly) who I'd had in mind when writing the male lead: Rutger Hauer. Rutger, Ann, Jack and I met one night at Barbara's house, and started talking about the script. This was not long after Rutger had done *Blade Runner*, so he was in demand as an actor and was incredibly charismatic in person. My chief memory of him, strangely enough, came to be his hands; they were immense, and when he shook my hand I think they covered my arm all the way to my elbow. Over the next few months, Rutger called me on the phone a few times to talk about the character and the script; he had some good notes that I worked to incorporate. And yes, it was kind of mind-boggling to pick up the phone and hear Rutger Hauer on the other end.

Jack started shopping *Lightning Strikes* around, and the response was disappointing: Everybody loved the script, but no one thought a female-driven action film would do well (even one famous female producer told us this).

Jack decided to try making a short film to help sell the script. By now Barbara Peeters had moved on, but *Lightning Strikes* soon acquired a new director...

Ron Cobb had originally been sought out for *Lightning Strikes* to design the hovertank, but after reading the script he begged for a shot at directing it. Cobb was the brilliant production designer of movies like *Alien* and *Conan the Barbarian*; before that, he'd been an astute and funny political cartoonist, and had even painted some of those *Famous Monsters* covers I'd gazed at so adoringly as a child. Ron had long wanted to direct; he'd actually been the first director assigned to *E.T.* until Spielberg had decided to take the project himself (and paid Ron off handsomely – Ron had a gorgeous house in Santa Monica that he called "The House That E.T. Built"). *Lightning Strikes* would be perfect for Ron – he could bring his amazing design skills heavily into play, but he also had an intuitive grasp of character and lots of energy. I adored Ron, and couldn't wait to get to work on his notes for the script.

While I did a new polish on the script per Ron's notes, Jack was assembling all the elements to make the short film. He got a permit to shoot in canyon tucked into the hills above Mulholland Drive; it was probably only a few hundred yards from houses in any direction, but somehow it looked isolated and wild. We made the front and side of the hovertank, complete with a hatch that would swing up, and mounted it onto a truck so it could move forward. We put together a crew and props and costuming. And one night we met up at the location, along with Ann, and shot the short film of *Lightning Strikes*. We even had a Steadicam operator, we fogged the area up, and Ron did a fantastic job directing.

In a few weeks the short was cut together, and Jack hired composer Richard Band to add a score. Richard had done lots of fun soundtracks for movies like *Re-animator*, and he turned in a fine score for our short.

Those of you who know anything about film production may be thinking by now, *But that sounds ridiculously expensive*...and you'd be right. It cost way more than I made in a year. Way more. The location shooting permit alone was a third of the budget and ran into five digits. Steadicam operators didn't come cheap. Neither did hovertanks, even only partial ones.

But I have to say...that short film of *Lightning Strikes* was fucking amazing. It was moody and exciting and tense and ultimately very heroic. It should have sold the project.

But it didn't. Jack spent a couple of years trying to find a buyer. He took that film everywhere. And heard the same stuff over and over and over again.

Nobody wanted a female action hero.

We finally all gave up and moved on. I squirmed in guilt over the amount of money Jack had sunk into *Lightning Strikes*, but managed to convince myself it wasn't really my fault.

And me...I got to say that I'd worked with Ron Cobb and been the amused recipient of late-night phone calls from Rutger Hauer.

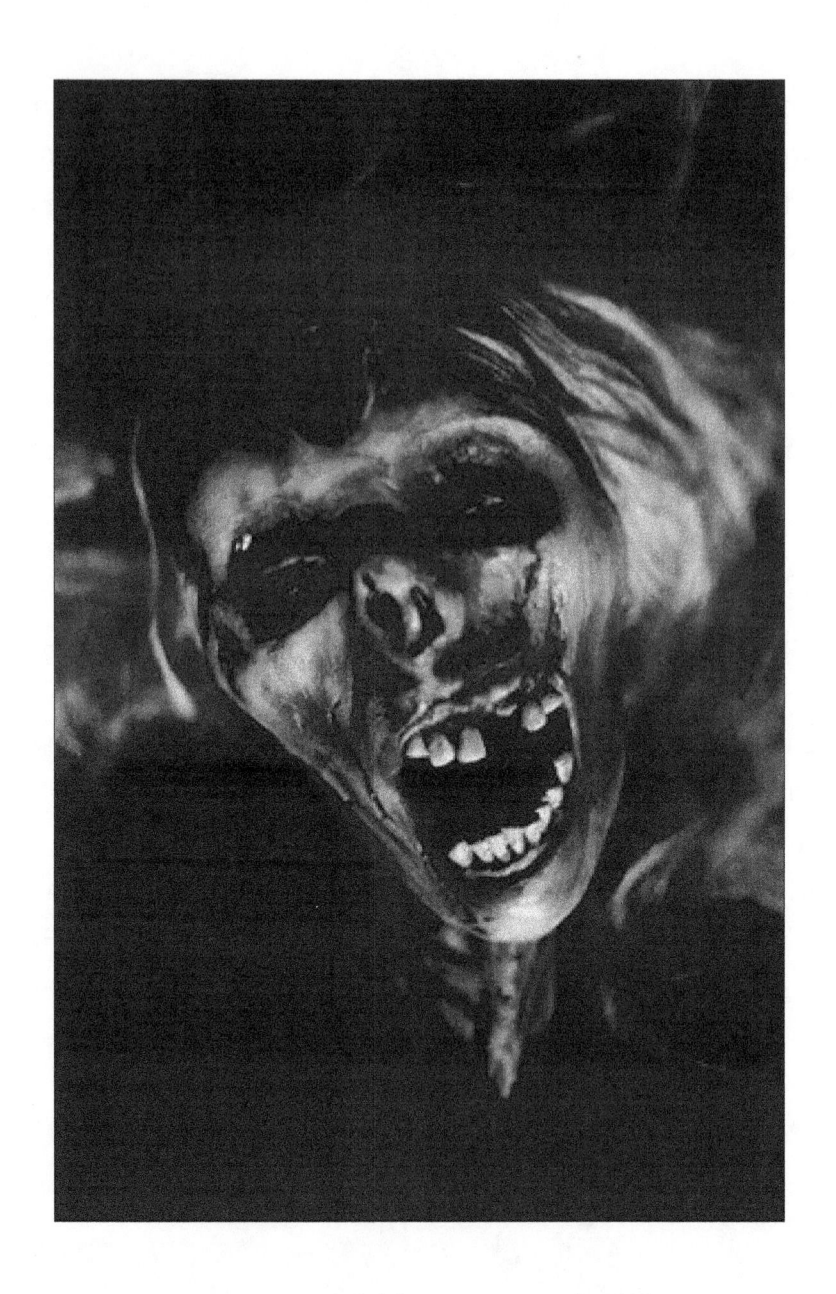

My corpse child from *One Dark Night*.

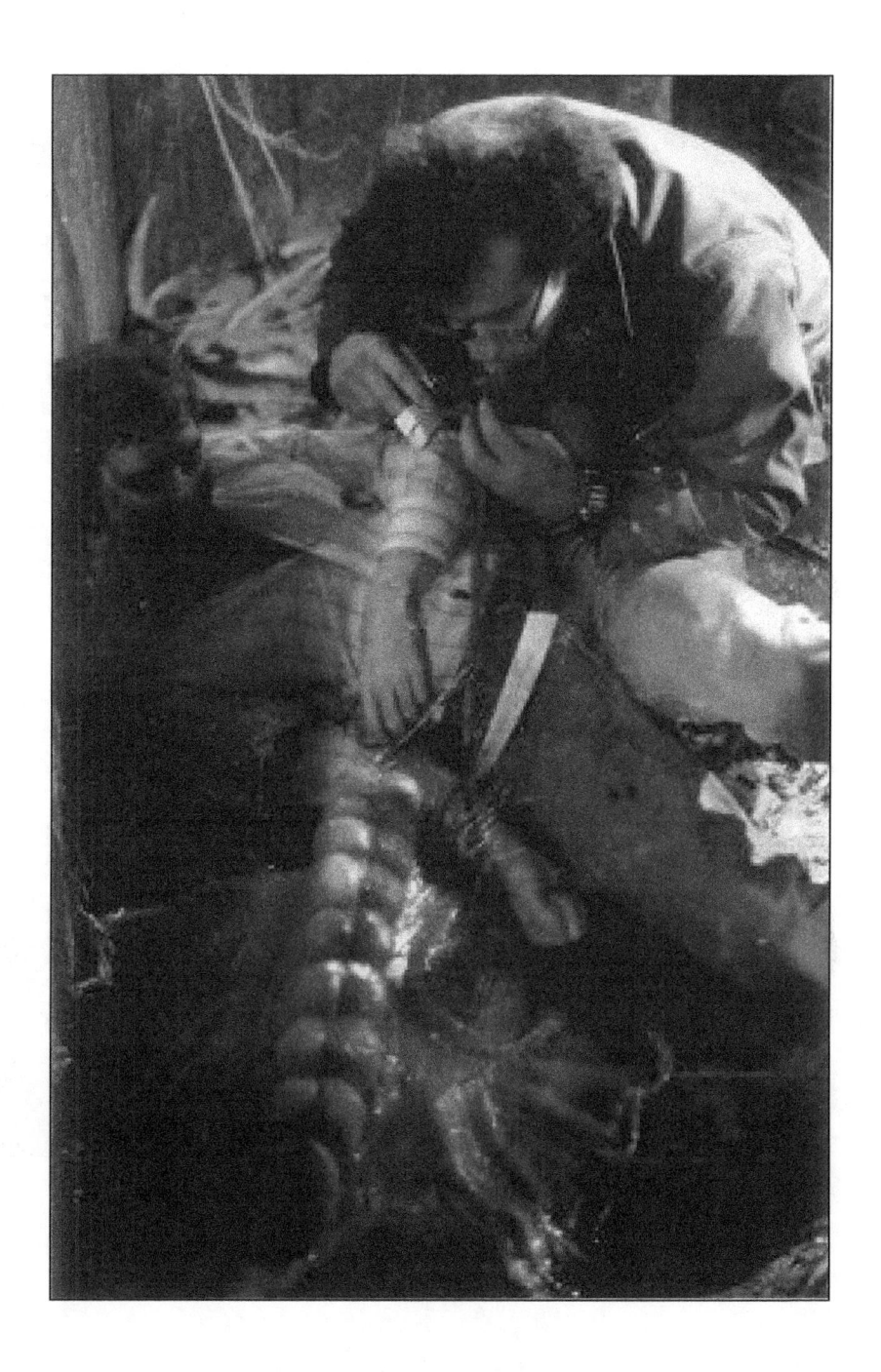

Bob Short trying to activate an uncooperative blood tube on the set of *Scared to Death* (aka *Syngenor*).

Ron Cobb directing the *Lightning Strikes* short.

From the *Lightning Strikes* short: The eponymous heroine saves an innocent she finds hanging from a tree.

Meet the Hollowheads: Greatest Hits

I'VE ALREADY WRITTEN AN ENTIRE BOOK about the making of my first film, *Life on the Edge* (released under the title *Meet the Hollowheads*), and put it up for free online at my website (www.lisamorton.com). It's a photojournal that I kept during the making of the film, and is illustrated with scads of photos I shot at the time.

However, I don't expect all of you to immediately rush to your computers and read that thing in its entirety, so I'm going to give you just the brief introduction and "greatest hits" moments.

In 1988, Tom Burman and I decided it was time to write a movie together. Tom had been through a lot of changes since *The Beast Within*: He'd divorced and remarried (to Bari Dreiband-Burman, an incredibly gifted make-up artist and fine artist), he'd moved the studio (to just a few blocks from where I've lived for the last twenty years), and he'd realized that he wanted to direct. I thought Tom would be a brilliant director, and so we started tossing ideas around. We finally settled on one that was essentially a strange parody of '50s sitcoms. I wrote a first draft, and passed it over to Tom, who was smart enough to throw out my entire second half (which followed teenaged brother and sister Bud and Cindy to a party) and fix the darn thing. Tom also brought a lot of the best dialogue to the script, and by the time he was done it was very close to the final shooting script.

We decided we'd try to make the film ourselves, with independent financing. We took a course on how to break down scripts and prepare budgets. We put together a detailed budget and shooting schedule. We thought we could make the movie on $350,000.

Enter John Chavez. John was a friend of mine who'd been doing small jobs around the periphery of the film industry for a while. He wanted to produce. He'd been talking to a new company who he thought would like the script. We agreed to let him attach himself as producer and take the script to his connections.

The company, Linden Productions, bought the script almost immediately. They also agreed to Tom as director, me as associate producer, and John as producer. Bari would also be an important part of the package, overseeing the Burman Studio and keeping us all on track.

If you don't know what an associate producer is, you're not alone. Here's the easiest definition: "Associate producer" is a title they give someone as kind of a gift. Usually that person does very little.

Tom Burman and I at the start of pre-production on *Life On the Edge*.

Unfortunately, in my case "associate producer" ended up meaning "the person who does all the crap jobs no one else will do."

Here, then, is my Greatest Hits list of moments from the making of *Life on the Edge*:

• Tom and I had captured some live toads from a stream in the hills north of the valley that he was going to turn into small creatures in the film. This meant we had to make tiny plaster casts of the toads. Tom reasoned that they spent a lot of time submerged in mud, and the plaster would be no different. So we submerged one of the toads in plaster – and the little fellow *cried*. I swear to God. Tom and I went pale, looked at each other, and Tom blurted out, "Oh my God, this is the most horrible thing I've ever done to another living creature." Fortunately, the toad was fine, the cast was good, and the toad creatures steal one scene in the movie.

• While shooting the same toads, I became the toad wrangler. No one else wanted to touch them. I not only didn't mind, but discovered they liked having their tummies stroked. By the way, when the movie was done we returned our toad stars to the wild. I'm sure they had interesting stories to share with their friends.

• We'd hired an unknown 14-year-old actress to play daughter Cindy. At one point Cindy, trying to decide what to wear to a party, had to parade about in a series of dresses, several of which were on the skimpy side. The poor kid burst into tears and ran from the set, until Tom coaxed her back. Her name was Juliette Lewis. I think she finally outgrew that crying-over-skimpy-clothing thing.

- I was assigned to puppeteer the family's pet, a large tentacle with a single eyeball on the end that lived in a tank in the living room. To do this, I had to crawl underneath the (barely) raised set, then sidle up into the tank, then squat there with my arm in the tentacle over my head, all while trying to hear Tom shout directions on the set. What none of us reckoned on was that this thing wasn't really built to last through four weeks of production, and by week two it was liquefying and releasing both noxious vapors and slimy crap into the tiny, enclosed tank space. One day shooting went on for a long time, I inhaled too much of the gas, and basically passed out. When I came to, I realized shooting had long ago wrapped and the entire crew had gone home, forgetting about the passed-out puppeteer in the tank. After that I demanded a fan and ventilation (I know, how prima donna-like of me, right?).

- We were shooting the "Edge Walk" sequence (which was later cut almost entirely from the film) when Tom suddenly dared me to play a hooker who would proposition the two 12-year-old boys. Of course I had to take that dare, so I was turned over to hair, make-up and wardrobe. An hour later I was a pale witchy-looking thing with blacked-out teeth, a massive teased 'fro, and a tight black outfit. The crew, of course, hooted and hollered when I walked in. The shoot went fine. And the studio gate guard propositioned me. I found that kind of icky, given what my teeth looked like. (And I am still credited at the end of the film as "Edge Slut", even though I was cut.)

- Remember how I said I got the jobs nobody else wanted? After we shot the scene in Billy's bedroom where the two young boys literally create a bloody mess destroying ticks they've removed from the dog, we knew we had to clean the set off in preparation for more shooting. So, while the rest of the crew broke for lunch, I spent hours scrubbing fake blood off pale blue walls.

- Because I have small hands, I ended up being cast in two amusing bits in the film: In one, I stood in for Richard Portnow in the scene when the villainous boss gets his fingers chopped off. I had the only hands small enough to fit into the prosthetic arm, so late one night I donned Richard's costume (which of course was amusingly huge on me), and we did the shot. The second time, you actually see my hands: In the opening montage, as John Glover makes a phone call that travels past a switchboard operator, those are my hands (with huge fake nails applied) that you see transferring tubes and wires.

- I absolutely loved our cast. John Glover goosed me and told me to read Elmore Leonard (John had been an absolutely loathsome villain in the film version of Leonard's *52 Pick-up*), Nancy Mette (playing the family mom) and I talked about my real mom, Anne Ramsey was incredibly sweet, despite suffering from a serious illness that would soon claim her life, and I adored our two young male leads, Matt Shakman and Joshua Miller. Matt's mom Inez and I became friends, and I stayed in touch with them for several years after *Edge* wrapped, even visiting Matt several times on the set of a sitcom he starred in called *Just the Ten of Us* (Heather Langenkamp from *A Nightmare on Elm Street* was one of Matt's co-stars; she was incredibly smart, and I liked bumping into her when I'd visit Matt). Joshua, of course, was the son of Jason Miller, star of *The Exorcist* and a Pulitzer Prize-winning playwright, and was a bright and interesting young man. I'm just sorry now that I hadn't yet seen Russ Meyer's *Faster Pussycat, Kill, Kill!*, because Josh's mother,

Susan Bernard, had been the young star of that film, which is now a favorite of mine.

The rest of *Meet the Hollowheads'* strange history isn't quite so fun. The film had minor success on the film festival circuit, but the first review (which was also the first review I'd ever received for anything) was an absolute disaster, and even attacked me by name (because of a silly quote from me in the presskitcalling the film "*Eraserhead* meets *Father Knows Best*" – the reviewer said I'd managed to insult both David Lynch and Robert Young). I'm not ashamed to confess that I actually placed that review in the kitchen sink and struck a match to it. It remains the worst review I've ever had; at least it could only go uphill from there.

The film didn't exactly lead to career success for anyone. Tom never directed again. Nancy Mette – who I thought was absolutely brilliant as Mom Hollowhead – never became a star. Linden Productions all but disowned the film (they eventually transformed into a non-profit organization that collects and catalogs atrocity footage from around the globe – I'm not sure if that includes *Meet the Hollowheads* or not). And heck, I couldn't even get an agent out of it.

But there've been fun things out of it, too. I've gotten some fascinating fan mail over the years, and it's always pleasing and surprising to find out people still like the film. One of my favorite encounters came in 2001, when UCLA was screening a Hong Kong movie I liked called *Fulltime Killer*. This film had been reviled by some Asian cinema fans on a certain message board I frequented at the time, but I'd stood up for it and indicated that I'd be happily attending the screening. Well, as I stood in the crowded lobby of the UCLA theater before the film, I suddenly heard a voice shout across the room, "Lisa Morton! You wrote *Meet the Hollowheads!*"

The voice happened to belong to Joey O'Bryan, the young American screenwriter of *Fulltime Killer*; he'd seen my posts on the forum, and happened to be a big fan of *Hollowheads*. We became very good friends as a result of that night.

Just since this year started, *Meet the Hollowheads* has appeared on Netflix Streaming, and suddenly I'm receiving more fan mail as a result. One fellow who works professionally in film restoration took my ancient ¾" tapes of the original cut and is working at his own personal restoration; another is preparing a 5,000-word essay for a film book. Every once in a while I get Google Alerts about folks posting links to my photojournal about the making of the film.

Personally, *Life on the Edge* now feels like something that happened to someone else. It was marred by personal tragedy for me (my stepfather, who I was close to, died unexpectedly two days before the start of principal photography), and of course its lack of success was disappointing. But I moved on, and I don't think much about it these days…

…until I get another fan letter.

Proof that *Meet the Hollowheads* really did receive a theatrical run… uh…somewhere.

A rare moment of fun on the set of *Adventures in Dinosaur City:* (Left to right) Director Brett Thompson, Shawn Hoffman ("Mick"), me, Tiffanie Poston ("Jamie"), Omri Katz ("Timmy"), and (kneeling) second unit cameraman Andreas Kossak.

Adventures in ~~Dumbass~~ – er, I Mean, Dinosaur City

AFTER LIFE ON THE EDGE WRAPPED, I headed off to try something I'd always wanted to experience: An archaeological dig. I spent a week uncovering an amazing Anasazi site near Springerville, Arizona. The dig was a wonderful experience and I'm glad I did it, but it also proved that archaeology wasn't for me – it was really hours of backbreaking work, squatting in dirt pits under a blazing sun or sorting dirt from treasures in these huge, heavy sifters. I was much more cut out for work that involved air conditioning and a comfortable chair.

I went onto *The Abyss*, and sometime near the end of that show I received a phone call one day from Glenn Jordan, who had composed the delightful score for *Edge*. Glenn told me that he'd just met with a company that was looking for a screenwriter for a children's fantasy that needed lots of crazy dialogue. Glenn mentioned me, and they asked if he could set up a meeting.

Smart Egg Pictures was a small production company that had recently scored a minor hit with a film called *Spaced Invaders*, a comedy about an alien invasion gone wrong that Disney had acquired. They had the track record and the connections now, and so they were anxious to get going on another children's film. The L.A. offices were headed by a half-Italian/half-Argentinian named Luigi Cingolani. Luigi was a handsome, enthusiastic madman with a thick accent and an ability to break me up into fits of laughter (an ability he seemed to greatly enjoy). Luigi would deliver wackadoodle lectures like this (remember the thick accent as you read this): "Some'a jobs need'a cock, some'a need a pussy. Director needs a cock. Script supervisor needs a pussy." Luigi had an Italian nickname for me, which he told me meant "little bird". His wife was a savvy, pretty blonde named Wili Baronet; she had this story idea involving talking dinosaurs. They wanted a writer to partner with Wili to write the script.

I met with Wili and we totally hit it off right away. I got the job almost immediately. The pay would be great (well, it was great... until the first production accountant decided to run off with the money and left me holding a bounced check), and after I told them that I could probably get them a fantastic art department and effects guys for cheap, they agreed to let me serve again as associate producer.

Wili and I started working on the script together. We had far too much fun, although it was also the first time I had to work on a computer, and that took more than a little getting used to. They were using Macs, which at the time were big, clunky things that weren't wildly easy to use; I remember once pressing a wrong key and deleting 40 pages of the script, which I had to just manually re-create from memory.

But the script was finished on time. *Dinosaurs!* would be a wacky children's fantasy about three kids who get sucked into an alternate dimension where dinosaurs walk and talk, while cavemen scheme to take over. The script had lots of crazy slanguage ("tailbrain" was a popular insult), and it was expensive but do-able, especially given the genius of the *Life on the Edge* art department, most of whom I brought on to *Dinosaurs!*.

Next up was finding a director. By now Luigi had taken a liking to me, and would ask for my advice on things...or, rather, he'd hope that I'd agree with a decision he'd already made. One day he showed me a short cartoon called *The Housekeeper*, and told me he was going to hire the guy – Brett Thompson – who'd made it, to be our director. "Uh....okay," I said. "But...uh...there's kind of a big difference between directing an animated short and a live action feature film, isn't there?"

Well, with these low-budget guys, hiring was all about how many things you could bring to a movie beyond what they were ostensibly hiring you for. I'd gotten in partly because of my art direction and effects connections; and because *Dinosaurs!* had one short animation scene, Luigi was figuring he'd get that cheap if he hired Brett to direct.

So I met Brett...and we both laughed when we realized we'd met before, years earlier, when Brett had sold me a rare poster. It also turned out that Brett had directed one other live action feature, a super-low-budget comedy called *Not Since Casanova* that was shot mostly in Brett's apartment and was tremendous fun. *Not Since Casanova* followed the adventures of a man-child named Prepski Morris who has befriended real-life legendary Disney artist Marc Davis (yes, Brett – aka "Brettski" – really was a close friend to Davis, and even took me over to the maestro's house on occasion, where I was pleased to also meet his lovely and talented wife Alice).

So, with a script and a director in place, things started to move quickly on *Dinosaurs!*, which was re-named *Adventures in Dinosaur City* when a television show called *Dinosaurs* debuted. A budget (2.5 million) was put together, a crew was hired, and a warehouse in the northern end of the San Fernando Valley was rented to serve as our little studio. We were soon installed there.

And that's when things started to go wrong. Before I'd started working in movies, I used to wonder how anyone could make a bad movie. By the time *Adventures in Dinosaur City* was over, I couldn't imagine how good movies ever got made.

Where to even start...well, Luigi and Wili were having (ahem) marital issues, which put me uncomfortably in between my co-writer and my producer. Luigi had hired a director of photography who had a superb resume as a special effects cinematographer (guess what deal Luigi was expecting here?), but had only done one other feature film. This guy was a perfectionist who worked slowly – great attributes for someone who expects to get in two or three effects shots in a day, but not so good when you need to pump through 35 or 40 live action set-ups. And sitting on top of it all was our line producer John Curran. John was a massive man who was an ex-Vietnam vet, and I've always gotten along well with military men (probably because my late stepfather had been a full lieutenant colonel in the Army), so I could easily work with him. He was experienced and connected, but also suffered from frequent migraines; half the time you'd go into John's office, it'd be pitch dark with all the windows blocked and the lights off, and he would grunt "yes" or "no" without even lifting his head.

Part of my job was going to be to supervise the Art Department. We had to build an entire fantasy world populated by humanoid dinosaurs and cavepeople on a small, tight budget, and it was gonna be tough. Fortunately we had almost exactly the same crew of guys we'd had for *Life on the Edge*, so they worked well together, and were innovative and tireless.

The real trouble set in about three days before shooting started. Brett has...well, let's just say an unfettered imagination, and when partnered with Luigi's recklessness, that was a recipe for disaster. "We need a scene where the kids are stuck on a runaway train that's going through underground lava caverns!" Brett would suddenly exclaim. Luigi would nod excitedly, then turn to me. "Write it, then add it to the Art Department's list." I would try to reason with him; the Art Department's budget was already stretched as thin as it would go, and this was an incredibly expensive proposition, one involving both miniatures and full-size sets. "No. Just do it," Luigi would respond. At that point, I would go off to John Curran, barge in on his darkened agony, and tell him what had just been ordered. He'd groan, and we'd waste two days trying to figure out some way to make it work ("well, maybe we could shift this money out of post-production...") before John finally put the kibosh on it. And we didn't have two days to waste.

Another brainstorm a few days before the start of production was to add a musical number. Yes, with an original song, singing, and choreographed dancing. At first I thought Brett was kidding, and late that night in an exhausted fit of bitter humor, I wrote a ridiculous song called "Hit Me Over the Head Again Darlin'", to be performed by a cavewoman chanteuse. It had lines like this:

Hit me over the head again, darlin',
Drag me all around by my hair.
Hit me over the head again, darlin',
And show me that you still care.

Well, Brett wasn't kidding. He grabbed those lyrics and gave them to his composer friend John Debney. A day later we had a song and I had a contract to sign for song lyrics (I confess I traded away publishing rights, although I think I may actually be listed as an ASCAP member or something). Brett brought in a friend who was a choreographer, and the musical number was shot.

(Later on, former Go-Go Jane Wiedlin was brought in to sing the song. Jane was reportedly offended by my sexist lyrics and rewrote the song to "Oh, I Love It When You Get Primitive, Darlin'". Thank God she was around to correct my well-known misogynist tendencies.)

And then there were the amusing small disasters. One day we had a meeting with the guys who were making the dinosaur suits and puppets. One of the three lead dinosaurs was a winsome little flyer named Forry (short for "rhamphorhynchoid", one of my favorite types of flying dinosaurs). Forry would be a bird-sized articulated puppet that could be hung from wires for flying shots. They'd painted him a lovely shade of blue.

"He's blue," I said, kind of shocked.

"Yeah...so?" answered the effects guys.

"Well, doesn't he have to be shot before a blue screen?"

This was back in the days before green screens; blue screens were still the standard for any shot in which an actor (or in this case, a puppet) had to be shot before a background image that would later be added in place of the blue. Part of the blue screen process was to remove anything that was blue from the shot; this was why actors shooting before a blue screen were always told they couldn't wear blue.

The special effects guys all stared at that goddamned blue puppet dumbfounded. John Curran kind of smirked. "She's right," he said, before turning to walk away. Needless to say, Forry had a new paint job by the end of the day.

The first day of shooting arrived…and by noon we hadn't gotten the first shot in yet. Five hours after the official start of principal photography on *Adventures in Dinosaur City*, and we were already behind schedule. That must've been some kind of record.

The film had been scheduled for a six-week shoot. By the end of the first week, we knew we were seriously deep in dinosaur doo.

As John Curran struggled to keep the whole thing from going up in an expensive tyrannosaurus-shaped mushroom cloud, I started a routine of working with our editor, an efficient and cool young lady named Liz Canney. Early every evening, Liz would get the previous day's footage in ("the dailies", as they're known in the biz lingo), and she and I would go over it together to make a list of everything that had been missed. And I'm not talking about "gee, it would be nice if" kind of shots; I'm talking about stuff that was needed to give this movie any possible iota of coherent story whatsoever. Really, we were running so slow that we'd often miss a full third of the shots we needed, and there was no time to re-shoot. So here's how it worked: Liz and I would make the list, then we'd figure out things that could conceivably be fixed with clever editing or dubbing, and then I'd take whatever was left and try to grab shots with a little second unit crew that Brett and I put together. So, while the main unit was filming on one end of the warehouse, I might be filming at the far end with just a cinematographer and maybe an actor or two.

Fortunately (amazingly), our young stars kept their enthusiasm for the project and graciously agreed to hang out after the end of their usual work day to help us grab these extra shots. Omri (Katz), Tiffanie (Poston), and Shawn (Hoffman) were all total troopers.

Which is what led to my meltdown on the set one night.

We'd been shooting something on the far end of the stage, but apparently the main unit's sound had somehow picked us up. One of the assistant directors promptly came striding furiously over in our direction, and proceeded to unleash a torrent of obscenity on the kids before turning around and proudly returning to the main crew.

Ask anybody who knows me, and they'll tell you that I'm usually a pretty calm individual. Reserved, even. But seeing this asshole unload on the young actors (I think Omri was all of 12 at the time – he'd gotten his mom to let him stay late for the extra shots) just popped my cork. I promptly followed him back to the other end of the warehouse and went ballistic on him in front of the entire crew. I'm not even sure what I said, but I'm sure it shocked the shit out of more than a few of those who heard it.

And it worked – he was incredibly nice to me and to the young actors for the entire rest of the filming.

As if it wasn't bad enough that I was dealing with shrieking crewmembers and watching this film spin completely out of control (and run roughshod over what had once been at least a decent kiddies' script), there was another aspect to this nightmare that just added to my stress levels: Sex. It was everywhere on this children's fantasy. There were at least two extramarital affairs going on around that warehouse, and more that weren't illicit, but weren't going well, either. Here I was pulling frequent all-nighters and 100-hour work weeks (I'm not exaggerating), and also finding myself in the middle of knowing about secret rendezvous and tete-a-tetes. I would say that unfortunately I wasn't getting any of this myself, except that none of these affairs ended well.

As we reached the midway point of production, I sometimes just stopped going home and stayed up all night on the set working. Now I'm not sure why I did that; I already knew this prehistoric turkey was beyond salvation. But I guess I had to try. It sure wasn't because it was fun.

And I kept getting roped into more and more jobs. I was an actor in a scene involving the parents and a science conference (and, for the second time in my acting career, my brilliant performance wound up on the cutting room floor). I even ended up one day in a huge rubber dinosaur suit that I couldn't see a damn thing out of, being asked to run along a narrow walkway with a drop of four feet on the side. I did it once, nearly plummeted, and promptly tore that goddamn head off and went on strike. I gained a whole new appreciation for extras that day, lemme tell ya.

Finally principal photography on *Adventures in Dinosaur City* wrapped, but my job was far from over: I would now be overseeing the miniatures crew that would occupy the warehouse for two weeks of effects shooting.

Even this relatively quiet part of the production held its share of small catastrophes. One day we were shooting a treehouse miniature that was supposed to be Forry's home; the miniatures crew had built a stunning model, one that was something like 20 feet in diameter, 6 feet tall, and filled with hundreds of tiny twinkling lights that gave it a lovely fairy tale quality. We would be shooting it with a motion control camera (they'd come a long way since the huge, clunky contraption I'd seen used on *Star Trek: The Motion Picture* and *Close Encounters*) that would be tracking slowly around the treehouse. We filled the area with fog and prepared to start the shot (which would take hours to complete, even though it would appear onscreen for only a few seconds).

"Something's wrong," I said.

I still kick myself for not being able to pinpoint it. Hey, I was working crazy hours, and my brain was a little fried. And – dammit, I was working with a bunch of professional effects cameramen who fucking did this for a living, but I guess they were all fried, too, because they just stared at me in incomprehension.

Well, I couldn't put my finger on it, so we finally let the shot run.

Duh. If you paid careful attention to my description of watching the motion control camera in action on *Close Encounters*, then you've probably already figured out what I missed that day:

We'd left the fucking air conditioning on in the warehouse.

Even though it was nowhere near the treehouse, and even though the fog looked immobile to the naked eye, the air conditioning was moving it ever so slightly. When spread out over the hours it would take to complete the shot...

Yep. When we got back the dailies, we had a shot of a beautiful, glittering treehouse, the camera making a dramatic track around it – while fog whipped by at hurricane speeds. It was completely unusable, and there was no time to try again. If you watch the finished film (and there's absolutely no reason you ever should), you'll see nothing but a still from this shot. It was all we could do.

The final debacle came on the last day. At the climax of the film's story, the bad guy's tower is blown up. We had a big miniature of the tower (again, about six feet tall), and we were going to blow that thing to bits while two cameras recorded it. We had an experienced pyrotechnics guy who'd done this a million times. I'd never seen a big explosion before, so I was curious. We placed our two cameras, I stood back about 30 feet, the charges were planted, we fired 'em off –

The explosion was so big it blew out part of the roof sixteen feet overhead.

One camera guy was only about ten feet away. We were all completely deafened, but I immediately ran up to him to be sure he was okay; fortunately he'd been behind heavy plastic sheeting. We were all fine...but that was one big effing hole in the roof. It blowed up reeeeeeaaallll good. What the hell...we were insured.

At the conclusion of the shoot, John Curran pulled me into his office for a double thank you. He asked me if I wanted any of the props from the film. We had a special remote control device that actually lit up and did all kinds of cool things, so I took that (I later re-used it in a science fiction play). Then he asked me what credits I wanted.

Well, aside from screenplay, of course, there was only one I really wanted: Second unit director. I was still thinking I might direct my own film someday, and I figured that might be a useful credit to have if that time ever came. It might be the biggest benefit I'd get out of this mess.

Of course it turned out to be the one credit I could not have; it'd already been promised to someone else. This was the low-budget switcheroo in reverse – instead of, "Hey, I'm hiring you to do Job A because I know you'll give me a great deal on Job B", this was a case of, "Hey, you give us a great deal on Job A, and we'll let you have a credit for Job B". John admitted that I definitely deserved that credit but there was nothing he could do about a deal that had been made months ago. At that point I didn't really care what they gave me. As it is, I received five credits on the film (for Screenplay, Associate Producer, Art Department Coordinator, Miniatures Coordinator, and Songwriter). Later on, when I finally showed the movie to my mom, she sat silently through the whole thing, then turned to me at the end and said, "Lisey, that was pretty bad."

"I know, Mom," I told her. "I just couldn't fix it."

"Well, why not? You had five credits on it." My worst nightmare had just been given voice. I think I cringed so hard I threw my back out.

Even after blowing the roof off the rented warehouse, I couldn't get away from *Adventures in Dinosaur City*. The first cut of the film was completed very soon after we wrapped, and it was (surprise!) awful. But of course rather than acknowledge that the film itself was bad, they did what they always do in Hollywood: They canned Liz Canney and brought in a new editor. Sure, that was all it would take to make this movie great!

Editor #2 was, admittedly, much more suited to the project. Peter Miller was a fast thinker with a wry sense of humor, and I was assigned to work with him on trying to make this dog bark. We spent weeks in the editing room rearranging scenes, going through extra footage, grabbing quick "insert" shots (little shots of inanimate objects), and looking for places where we could dub in new lines. Peter was a master at finding just the right spot where he could cut away from a character who'd been speaking, and we could write new lines that the actor would add during dubbing, which was still to come. We actually did manage to cover a few of the massive plot holes in this fashion, and there's no question that Peter made the film better (and yes, I know that if you've actually seen the film, right now you're thinking, Wait – it was even WORSE at one point? Yes. Really it was).

To score the film, Luigi found a talented young composer named Fredric Teetsel. He of course hired Fredric because (no! really?!) he could bring something else to the film; in this case, that something else was a full orchestra. Fredric started coming up with themes, but Luigi hated all of them. "No," he'd just say over and over, "I want Danny Elfman." He pounded "Danny Elfman" into poor Fredric so much that he finally got what he wanted, and *Adventures in Dinosaur City* bears a score that sounds like it was lifted out of a Pee-Wee Herman movie. It's still one of the few good things about the movie.

Dubbing was completed, and finally it came to the last of the sound: The sound effects. I was there on the day that sound effects recording was to commence. We were in a cool post-production studio in Burbank, just Luigi and me and a couple of sound effects experts. Just when the work was about to start, John Curran showed up and said something to Luigi. Luigi went nuts.

It turned out there was, very simply, no money left in the budget for sound effects. They'd shuffled that part of the budget around to cover other things; Luigi had believed he'd be able to cajole a few extra bucks out of Smart Egg's owner, a guy who sold cars in Eastern Europe. There was just enough money for a few stock sound effects; there would be no original sound effects created for this film set in a fantasy world.

But the good news was: It was officially done.

A few weeks later, the first test screening was held at a theater in Santa Monica. It was a matinee. They'd made sure the theater was packed with kids.

Amazingly enough, the kids seemed to enjoy it. But most of their parents were in the lobby long before it was over.

That night, I received a late phone call from Luigi. He was gloating. "You see? The kids, they'a love it!"

"Yeah, Luigi, but," I answered, "wouldn't it have been better to have made a movie that their parents could actually sit through, too?"

That did it. "Oh my God," Luigi began muttering, "oh my God. You are right. Oh my God. What are we going to do? Oh my God."

I had no answer for that.

Needless to say, the film did not get the theatrical release that *Spaced Invaders* had enjoyed. It did, however, get picked up by the Disney Channel, and at one point it was actually the top Blockbusters rental for children. It even inspired a videogame called *Dinocity*. According to imdb.com, there was once a Myspace fan group for the film. Of course these imdb users are the same brainiacs who claim that we were all sitting around during the making of the movie thinking, "Oh man this movie is going to be so great! EVERYBODY is going to love it!!"

A few years after *Adventures in Dinosaur City*, Luigi left the movie biz and went into banking. He and Wili divorced, and with her new husband Wili became a successful television producer. Brett directed one more feature – a documentary called *The Haunted World of Edward D. Wood Jr.* – and he and I later became a writing team. And as for me...well, the bad news is that *Adventures in Dinosaur City* was basically my swan song to film production. This thing had exhausted me and left me with a product that I was all but completely ashamed of. Never again would I work insane hours on bullshit that I knew would suck. Even though *Adventures in Dinosaur City* paid me enough to live off for a year, I decided that if I ever did another film, I would write the screenplay, take the money, and run away. Fast.

The good news is that the dual failure of both *Life on the Edge* and *Adventures in Dinosaur City* made me anxious to see my name on something I could actually be proud of, and I began to consider that there might be other things I could write that didn't begin with the words "FADE IN".

Shawn and Tiffanie wisely stay back to avoid the dinosaur/caveman rumble.

John Martin and Marybeth DeLucia in *Sane Reaction*.

David LaPorte as Philip K. Dick and Esther Williams as Sadassa Silvia in *Radio Free Albemuth*

The Play's the Thing...
to Make You Crazy, I Mean

AFTER THE GREAT DINOSAUR DEBACLE, I was in a strange place. I had enough money to live on for at least a year (if I lived somewhat frugally), but no idea what I'd do at the end of that time. And I wasn't even sure what I wanted to do before that. After *Dinosaur City*, I knew that I never again wanted to work on a film, at least not as anything less than a director. If I was the one at the top (the one with a cock, according to Luigi), then maybe it would be different...but I was never again going to bust my ass doing grunt work on movies that were destined to fail.

I would also be happy to sell screenplays, but – even after having had two feature films produced – that hadn't gotten any easier. I still had no agent, and the companies that had made *Life on the Edge* and *Adventures in Dinosaur City* were both almost out of business (there was in fact some talk of writing something else for Smart Egg, but it never happened). My services weren't exactly in high demand.

Well, what the hell...this was every writer's dream, right? To be able to live from writing income alone, without the messy distractions of some day job? So fine. I'd be a writer. I'd write screenplays like crazy. I'd shop them to agents until something clicked. I'd write my ass off.

Except I didn't.

I am here to tell you, my writing brothers and sisters, that living as a full-time writer may not be all it's cracked up to be. I was bored, lonely, and still recovering from the exhaustion of working on *Dinosaur City*. The writing went slower than it had ever gone. I started things I never finished. They sucked. I tried to schedule my days carefully, but it didn't work. I started to sleep more and more, and leave the apartment less and less. Whenever I did, I had an uncomfortable sort of tunnel vision – nothing seemed to come into focus or be quite real. I needed something or I was going to go nuts.

During this time, one thing I involved myself more in was small theater. Just after finishing *Life on the Edge*, Tom's actor son Barney had asked us if we'd both like to be involved in a Halloween show his theater company was putting on. At that point I knew nothing about local theater beyond a few shows I'd seen (and I think the last show I'd seen had been a production of *The Only Game in Town* with Kenneth McMillan; I was there with Paul, who'd worked with McMillan on *A Death in Canaan*, and afterward we chatted about *Dune*, which McMillan had just finished filming). I was curious, and was offered an opportunity to write a short horror play for the evening. I chose to adapt a vampire story by August Derleth called "The Drifting Snow" (this was back before we all worried endlessly about copyright stuff). Tom adapted and directed Edgar Allan Poe's "The System of Doctor Tarr and Professor Fether", about lunatics who have taken over an asylum. The evening, called Neo-Gothic Theatre, was hardly a resounding success, but I liked the company (Theatre of N.O.T.E., which stood for "New One-Act Theatre Ensemble") and thought it might be a good way to get my feet wet as a director.

I went off and had my dinosaur nightmare. Not long after that finally wrapped, I saw a new full-length work N.O.T.E. had produced called *Sombrero Fallout,* based on the book of the same name by Richard Brautigan. I liked the production, and started to think about adapting something by my favorite writer Philip K. Dick. I knew most of Dick's works would be tied up in endless film options, but there was one book I loved which was considered a lesser-known work, which I'd never heard being considered for film, and which I thought would work well on stage: *Radio Free Albemuth*. N.O.T.E. was intrigued enough to offer me some help in obtaining the rights, and to my surprise Dick's agent agreed immediately to the terms we offered. Because I would need to cast a number of key roles from outside N.O.T.E.'s small and largely youthful pool of talent, N.O.T.E. wouldn't offer me the use of their theater on weekends, but gave me the space during mid-week.

I adapted the novel into a full-length play, and we started casting. *Radio Free Albemuth* is one of the novels from the later period of Dick's life (post-1972), when he became obsessed with a god-like concept he called "VALIS", or "Vast Active Living Intelligence System". *Albemuth* is usually considered little more than practice for the novel *Valis*, but I stand alone in thinking *Albemuth* is actually the better book. It depicts an alternate America ruled by a charismatic but tyrannical president named Ferris Fremont, and much of it is bitterly funny. The lead characters are Philip K. Dick and his best friend Nicholas Brady, and the plot centers on their efforts to survive Fremont's increasingly fascistic state. For Brady, I thought Paul would be perfect, and he'd never done as much theater as he'd wanted to; he agreed immediately. For Phil, I held auditions and cast a wonderful actor named David LaPorte, who would remain a friend for some time. One amusing member of the cast (playing an FBI agent) was Hy Pike, who had played bar owner Taffy Lewis in *Blade Runner*; he was my producer's next door neighbor, and my inner fan (*Blade Runner* is one of my top three or four favorite movies) was pleased to have him in my Dick adaptation.

This would be my first real workout as a director, and the rehearsals went, for the most part, smoothly. N.O.T.E.'s theater was a very odd space tucked away on a side street in Hollywood (it has since relocated to much better digs); there was an Armenian bakery at the front of the building, and an honest-to-goodness sweatshop above it (with rows of ancient sewing machines and everything). The dressing rooms were an alley; the lobby was a sidewalk. The advantages, however, were a two-story stage (which I made use of, staging Fremont's speeches on the upper level), and a good tech booth located at the back of the theater (I decided to run lights and sound myself during the production and had already learned how to run the lighting "dimmer board" and the sound system).

The cast on *Albemuth* was a dream. They were committed and hard-working, two attributes I would miss on other productions; they made it easy for a first-time director. We approached opening night confident that we had a provocative, challenging, unusual show on our hands. I knew Dick had spent the last years of his life only about thirty minutes south of us, and I hoped to see his friends and family members in the audience.

Well, as it turned out, I would have been glad to have seen *anyone* in the audience. I mean, *nobody* came to see *Radio Free Albemuth*. Sure, we were running mid-week and the Persian Gulf War broke out a week before we opened, but still, I expected someone to see it. We got two reviews, one that was pretty bad and one that was merely lukewarm. Only one of Dick's friends – Doris Sauter, who'd served as the basis of the character "Sadassa Sylvia" in Albemuth – came to see the play, which she thankfully praised highly in *The Philip K. Dick Society Newsletter*. Years later, I'd meet other friends of Dick's who all told me that they'd avoided seeing it for fear that it would be bad, and by the time they heard it was good, it had ended its run.

It may not have been successful, but *Radio Free Albemuth* was one of the best experiences of my life. I sat in the booth night after night, marveling at how well I thought it had come together. I remain very proud of it today.

I did a few other small shows here and there, but nothing major happened until 1992. I wasn't happy with N.O.T.E., and an actress friend of David LaPorte's ended up steering me to a company in West L.A. she belonged to: The Zeitgeist Theatre Company. I attended one of their workshops, and almost instantly felt much more at home; they lacked the sort of pretentiousness that I felt was present in much of N.O.T.E.'s other work, and they had a large and friendly group of talented actors. I joined up right away, and started workshopping a new short one-act play called *Sane Reaction*.

I didn't know it at the time, but *Sane Reaction* would change my life.

Zeitgeist was run by a huge ex-Philadelphia native named John Martin, who wrote and directed most of the company's shows as well as starring in them. But John couldn't write enough to keep everyone in Zeitgeist working, so he was receptive to having another writer in the group. He was planning an evening of one-act plays to open in December of 1992, and still needed two pieces to make a full slate. I quickly wrote a comedic sketch called *What a Riot*, while *Sane Reaction* would be the final show in the evening.

Sane Reaction is a thriller about a woman who has picked up a man she doesn't know at a party and brought him back to her place, only to discover that he's a serial killer. That, mind you, is only the first half, as the play takes a serious left turn at the midway point. A "two-hander" (meaning a play with only two characters), nearly every actor in Zeitgeist wanted the man's role, but John claimed it for himself. The woman's role would be split between two actresses, MaryBeth deLucia and Kate McBride. I would direct and also run lights and sound.

Opening night of *Twisted Romance* was unforgettable. John had a large and devoted following, and the theater was sold out. The first four plays in the evening went well, and the audience applauded enthusiastically at the close of each one.

Then we got to *Sane Reaction*. The audience sat quietly through the performance. At the end of the play, I slammed the lights abruptly to black, then listened for that gratifying round of applause –

It didn't come. There was silence. Total silence. I mean, you could hear a fucking pin drop down there.

My heart sank. I'd thought rehearsals had gone so well. I thought it was something really special.

Then I brought the lights up, took one look at that audience, and saw the truth: They were in shock. That goddamn play had absolutely traumatized them.

As the actors came onstage to take their bows, that applause started – and it was thunderous now. They hooted, they hollered. They fucking loved *Sane Reaction*. They had been shown something they'd never seen in a theater before, and now that they understood that, they ate it up.

Sane Reaction proceeded to sell out its entire run and receive 100% rave reviews. The *L.A. Times* called it "deliciously macabre" and said it took "*Extremities* to extremes." The *LA Weekly* said it "contains moments of incredibly uncomfortable tension", and the *LA Reader* said, "Morton springs her deceptively casual script with the precision of a mousetrap. She expertly manipulates the play's emotional shifts, from terror to humor and then to perverse satisfaction…" The play's run was extended. Later, *Sane Reaction* would also be produced in San Francisco and New York. And in 1993, *Sane Reaction* became the basis of a short story which would be my first professional fiction sale (to *Dark Voices VI*, edited by Stephen Jones and David Sutton).

Sane Reaction was probably the first time in my creative life that I felt I'd finally gotten it right. Not only had I enjoyed putting it together, but audiences and critics loved it, too. It gave me real confidence in my ability to direct, and re-inspired me as a writer.

After *Sane Reaction*, I did a number of other, smaller shows with Zeitgeist, then was approached by my friends Rocky and Jill Heck with an interesting proposition: They wanted to form a theater company dedicated to producing genre works, and they wanted to call it Theatre Phantastique.

Well, you know I had to be all over that. We started talking about what we would do for an initial outing, and decided on an evening that would mix original and adapted material, and one-acts and monologues. Rocky and I would split writing, directing and producing duties, and we'd both have a hand in the expenses. Rocky's wife Jill would oversee other aspects of the show, like promotion and design, and we'd cast the show with actors who were talented enough to appear in more than one piece.

Rocky and I each picked works to adapt, and we were fortunate enough to obtain rights: Rocky chose Dennis Etchison's *The Dead Line*, Kim Newman's *The Man Who Collected Barker*, and Kristine Kathryn Rusch's *Choosing a Weapon*. I adapted Theodore Sturgeon's *The Graveyard Reader*, and also provided two original monologues ("The Territorial Imperative" and "I'm Not Norman"), and one original play, *Savings and Lones*.

For the cast, we held no auditions, but instead chose our actors from those we'd worked with successfully in other productions. Paul worked in three of the shows, David LaPorte and MaryBeth DeLucia each appeared in one, and a guy from Zeitgeist named Lonnie Schuyler came on board to both act and direct (Lonnie directed "The Territorial Imperative" and directed and starred in *Savings and Lones*).

I'd met Lonnie through Zeitgeist when he starred in the white trash comedy *What a Riot* for me, and I was impressed by his energy, his desire to learn and to work, and his stage presence. We worked well together, feeding off each others' ideas, and Lonnie's life story intrigued me as well: His mother had worked as a stripper, and he'd briefly followed in her footsteps by working as a male stripper. He was too smart to stay in that arena for long, though, and soon found his way to Southern California. With his charisma and charm, it was only a matter of time before Lonnie would find work in Hollywood.

As a sort of ridiculous in-joke, we named our evening of horror plays *Life on the Edge* (hahaha, right?), then tacked on the sub-title *Tales of Urban Horror*. Rocky and Jill ended up sinking lots of money into it.

And it flopped.

Once again, nobody came. I mean, it wasn't the total no-show disaster that *Albemuth* had been, but it came nowhere near recouping even a fraction of the dough that'd been poured into it. Reviews were tepid – actually they were pretty good for my pieces, especially "The Territorial Imperative", a blackly comedic monologue about a man obsessed with hunting cockroaches – but mixed on the whole evening.

Before we'd quite figured out just how much money we'd lost, though, we still had thoughts of future productions for Theatre Phantastique, and one night we'd held a reading which would prove to be strangely important for me: The play was called *Marionette*, and it was based on a short story Rocky had found by a woman named Roberta Lannes. Roberta had been a student in a writing class Dennis taught at UCLA, and I think Dennis had suggested that we should look at her work. She'd been excited by the prospect of working in theater, and had tried her own adaptation.

Well, the reading didn't go incredibly well, but I clicked with Roberta right away on an absurdly deep level. We soon became best gal pals, and remain that way 20 years later. I still credit Roberta with launching my fiction writing career.

But unfortunately I couldn't launch Roberta's playwriting career – after one production, Theatre Phantastique was dead and buried.

I wanted to do another full-length show of my own, and I wrote an epic, three-act science fiction comedy called *Trashers*. I took it to Zeitgeist and started workshopping it. John Martin and I talked a lot about staging it, but things started going wrong at Zeitgeist. For me it came to a head on the night that I was running lights and sound, brushed against a cable, and received a shock strong enough to throw me across the room. The Burbage was falling apart (and indeed, it was shortly converted to office space).

Lonnie suggested he and I form our own theater company. We could have all the control that way. We could do the plays we wanted, in a space we liked. We could eventually do *Trashers* right.

I agreed with him. We soon found a fantastic theater in the valley called the Lionstar; the fellow who owned it was a wonderful guy named Anthony who gave us a great deal on renting the space. We could actually afford to do this. We named our new company First Stage Alert, invited our favorite actors to join us, and set up shop.

For our first production, we decided to do an evening of four horror one-acts; we'd run it around Halloween, and call it *Spirits of the Season*. We themed the evening as contemporary takes on four classic monsters – the vampire, the werewolf, the ghost, and the zombie – and I wrote four original one-acts to fill those slots. We'd assembled a fine company of actors, and so we rotated casts to give everyone a chance to work.

Unlike poor *Life on the Edge: Tales of Urban Horror*, *Spirits of the Season* was a complete hit. Audiences loved it, critics loved it, and we extended its run…twice. The *L.A. Times* said it "isn't some dumb ghoul show, but a collection of pieces riddled with disturbing thoughts", and the *LA Weekly* said it "score(d) a stake to the heart".

Spirits of the Season had given us a fine first production for our new venture. The future of First Stage Alert seemed bright.

Of course you know how that always goes.

Our next production was a full-length play: *Hello, Bob!* was the West Coast premiere of a play by major award-winning playwright Robert Patrick, and I admit that I was initially against doing it. I was nervous about *Hello, Bob!* because this guy Patrick was a big deal, and because I'd had nothing to do with setting up the deal with him – would he be a prima donna? Would he want scads of money we didn't have, or artistic control? Would he drive us all crazy(er)?

Well, Bob (yes, that is his name in the play's title) turned out to be great to work with, and he and I even became friends for a while. *Hello, Bob!* was a follow-up to Bob's Broadway production *Kennedy's Children*, and like that play it was presented as a series of interconnecting monologues. Bob even wanted me to play one, about an Irish photographer whose lover had been killed by the IRA.

Now, I wasn't really an actress, of course (despite my magnificent performance as the Edge Slut in *Life on the Edge*), but I liked Bob and wanted to honor his wishes. We had a regular actress doing that part, but I learned it as well (complete with Irish accent), and I surprised Bob by doing it one night when I knew he was in the audience. It was, of course, nerve-wrenching, but it was actually fun, too, and I think I pulled it off. Bob seemed pleased afterwards, and although I wasn't exactly bitten by the acting bug, I knew I could do something more complex if I ever had to.

After *Hello, Bob!* ended, we started trying to decide on our next production. Suddenly, I found myself in demand as an animation writer, and I told Lonnie I'd have to step back from First Stage Alert for a while to make some money.

Things didn't go well in my absence.

I can't really say exactly what happened, because I wasn't there…but the next thing I knew, Lonnie was making his own low-budget feature called *Odds and Ends*, and he'd promised parts to all of the actors in our company. I'm not clear on what happened to the company's funds, but somehow the entire company seemed to have approved of Lonnie's decision to apply the money to his film. Lonnie was also starting to have...well, let's say temper issues. I got a panicky call one day from an actress who said he'd threatened her with a pair of scissors. I got off lucky – he only threw pillows at me.

First Stage Alert was done. *Odds and Ends* was unwatchable. Lonnie got a part on an Aaron Spelling show called *Models Inc.*, but it was canceled after one season. He finally left L.A. for Iowa, where he's still making his own movies.

You'd think I would have washed my hands of theater after that, but I still had *Trashers* lurking there at the edge of my consciousness, forever poking its little android hands into my gray matter and saying, *Produce me...*

At some point in 1999, I found out that Zeitgeist had relocated, and was now working out of a theater just a few blocks from where I lived. I checked it out, and found that John was open to doing *Trashers*. The space was very small, and I knew it would be tough to stage the show properly there, but a couple of the actors were into it, and I had to try it, after all these years.

I should have called it quits during rehearsals. Sure, some of the actors were committed...but others just didn't show up for rehearsals, or bother to memorize their lines – or tell me until a week before opening that they couldn't make the first two weeks' performance. Fortunately, that particular role was the only one in the show that I was remotely right for, so I figured I would just take that role for the first two weekends (what the hell, I knew the lines and the blocking, right?). I wouldn't be running lights and sound this time around – John Martin was doing that – so it shouldn't be a problem.

Except it was. Everything was a problem on *Trashers*. The set was a disaster; John had actually tried to construct a high-tech futuristic office out of leftover bathroom linoleum. Half the cast was unprepared by opening night. Even parking was a problem.

Opening night, the same critic from the *Times* who had given me the rave for *Spirits of the Season* was there. I hoped he'd remember me from that show. I thought maybe he might look past the obvious production problems with *Trashers* and praise the script.

Boy, was I wrong. He annihilated *Trashers*. I think he actually said it set all small theater in Los Angeles back. Or something like that.

But *Trashers* was about to get even worse: Mere moments before the Sunday matinee, John told me he couldn't run the lights and sound that day. And then he left.

Uhhhh…there was no one else who could do it. And I was onstage performing…how was that going to work?

I had about a frantic thirty minutes to come up with a solution, and come up with one I did: I actually ran back and forth to the lighting booth, running the lights and sound before returning to stage. I incorporated this action into some hastily-rewritten lines and blocking. A couple of lines I even just yelled from the booth. In the end, it worked out okay…but I still wanted to murder John.

Trashers was the theatrical equivalent of *Adventures in Dinosaur City*, except that it was worse in one enormous way: I still loved the fucking thing. The script part, I mean. Not the production. That production broke my heart.

For a while afterward, I actually toyed with the idea of turning *Trashers* into a low-budget film. I reconnected briefly with a couple of the art department guys from *Life on the Edge* and *Dinosaur City*, and they thought they could make the sets cheap; they even had a small studio where we could shoot. But in the end I abandoned the idea because I knew I couldn't stand watching my baby potentially go up in flames twice. Someday I might turn *Trashers* into a novel... although I don't think the world of science fiction would know what to make of it.

It's now been more than a dozen years since *Trashers*, and people still ask me if I'm doing theater these days. I always just politely shake my head and tell them "no", when what I really want to say is that I'd cut off some of my own body parts and then eat them raw before I'd ever do theater again. Did I forget to mention that I'd also sunk thousands of dollars into *Trashers*? It took me years to pay that credit card off, and what had it all been for? The privilege of being crucified in the *Times* and watching a play I knew was good and innovative get destroyed live before my eyes.

Sorry, theater lovers, but...never again.

AGE
ABRAMS/GENTILE
ENTERTAINMENT INC.

Sky Dancers™

Writer's Bible Rev. 003
6/8/95

244 WEST 54TH STREET, 9TH FLOOR, NEW YORK, N.Y. 10019
TEL (212) 757-0700 FAX (212) 765-1597

The *Sky Dancers* bible.

Promotional pamphlet for *Van-Pires*.

Agents: Bloodsucking Leeches from Hell, or Bloodsucking Leeches from Heaven?

AGENTS. THEY CAN MAKE OR BREAK A WRITER. Well, okay – so far they've mainly done the breaking part for me, but I have it on good authority that they make lots of other writers.

I've always thought of agents as some sort of big speakeasy: They're this magical place that I can stand outside of and hear everyone laughing and having a great time inside, but nobody's ever given me the right password to get in. C'mon, guys…I just want a drink. Doesn't have to be an expensive one, even. Just a sip of bad beer will do.

Here's how it should go (and how common mythology suggests it does go): Talented young writer pens a kickass script and comes to Hollywood. Writer gets the Writers Guild's list of agents (or some other list) and starts writing query letters; meanwhile, writer also starts hanging out at industry hangouts, in hopes of bumping into agents. Either a query letter pays off or writer gets lucky and bumps. Writer lands great agent, who proceeds to land great deal for script.

So, there I was in the '80s, writing screenplays that people like Ron Cobb and Rutger Hauer and Tom Burman were digging, and I was getting nowhere with agents. I'd send out masses of query letters, and would receive zero – yes, ZERO – responses. I once had a mutual friend get a mid-level agent to look at a script, and the mid-level agent at least did write me back…only to accuse me of having stolen the entire script from a book I'd never heard of (and which, when I did look up said book, of course bore almost no resemblance to my script).

Then *Life on the Edge* happened, and I thought, *People have told me for years that the agents would come to me when I finally sold a script, so c'mon, boys and girls – get in line, I'm ready!*

Of course no agents came after me. Hell, they still wouldn't answer queries.

Next came *Adventures in Dinosaur City*. There I was on a Friday afternoon with a contract literally in hand for a fairly significant amount of money, and it had to be signed and returned on Monday. I needed an agent to go over this. I made frantic phone calls. I finally found a guy who was at a good agency who said he'd take a look. I dropped a copy off for him.

I waited two hours…and then he called me and said he couldn't do it because he had "a personal connection with Wili Baronet" (Wili was my co-writer on the film). Later on, when I asked Wili, she of course told me she'd barely met the man once, and had no idea what he was talking about. I believed her.

Instead I found a great attorney, Howard, who went over the contract carefully for me, explained things to me, and fixed a couple of clauses. Howard was young, hip and very successful – he had offices in what was popularly called "the Die Hard building", because it was the big tower in Century City where the film had been shot. Fine, I thought, I'll just use an attorney and screw these agents.

But there was no escape. After I finished *Dinosaur City*, a friend told me he'd just met an agent who he thought I'd love, and she'd actually loved *Life on the Edge*. What the hell…sure, I'd meet with her.

Well, I adored S. And yes, I'm only going to use her first initial, S. And if you think that means things didn't turn out well...you've gotten to know me by now, haven't you?

S. signed me right away. She had a small "boutique" agency and only handled a few clients, but her Hollywood offices were nice, she and I had a pleasant, easy chemistry, and – best of all – she said I was the type of writer who she could get work for almost instantly.

The thing is...she was right. She sent me out on my first meeting days after signing me, and I got the job. It was re-writing an animated feature for an independent production company. It would pay $15,000 – not quite what I'd made on *Dinosaur City*, but it'd be a whoooooooooole lot less stressful and over quickly.

I was on Cloud Nine. This was finally it. I had a real honest-to-God agent. I'd nabbed the first thing she sent me out on.

Maybe I really could make a living doing this.

I'd never written for animation before, but fortunately the company had already hired a director who was a former animator with an extensive background, and he patiently schooled me in the special requirements of animation writing. The script proceeded well. Both director and producer were happy with the increments I was giving them.

The only fumble came the day I delivered the script, one day before my deadline. I proudly set my baby down on the producer's desk. He stared at it, then – without even opening it – looked up at me and said, "It can't be any good."

"Why not?" I asked. I mean, he hadn't so much as riffled the pages.

"Because you rushed it."

Now, this would be an exceedingly witty comment if he hadn't been serious. But he was. Serious, I mean, not witty. And I suddenly understood all the stories I'd heard about screenwriters "missing" deadlines. It wasn't because they were lazy or slow; it was because they already knew what I was still learning: That producers were insane.

Anyway, they were happy enough with the draft to pay promptly. In case you're not familiar with how payments work with agents, here's a crash course: Checks go to your agent first, who cashes them and then writes you a check for the amount less the agent's commission.

So I waited for the check to come from my spanky new agent. I waited…and waited…

Here's roughly how it went:

WEEK #1 – S. says company still hasn't paid.

WEEK #2 – S. says company finally paid, but something was wrong with the check. She's asked for a new check.

WEEK #3 – S. says she still hasn't gotten the new check.

WEEK #4 – S. says something happened with the new check in the mail.

WEEK #5 – S. says someone stole the new check from the mail. She's trying to straighten it out.

WEEK #6 – S. says someone just walked into a bank and cashed the new check. *My* new check.

Okay, I'm a little slow. Hey, so crucify me; I always prefer to believe the best about people. And I'm not completely stupid – I knew something was wrong with S.'s story by Week #3, but I just wasn't sure what to do. But by the time she got to the impossible – someone who wasn't me cashing my check – I knew something really, really bad was going on.

I called the company and asked when the check had been cashed. They told me the day after they'd sent it. I asked whose signature was on it. S.'s, of course. I asked if they could give me a copy of the cashed check. They did. Sure enough, there was S.'s signature and date stamp from six weeks ago.

I immediately called Howard, my hip attorney. Howard asked me to fax the check copies to him. I did. Fifteen minutes later, Howard faxed me a copy of a letter he'd just faxed to S., giving her 24 hours to respond.

S. called and asked if we could meet for lunch at a nearby restaurant. An hour later, she was sitting across from me sobbing about the IRS and ex-husbands and various assorted other money problems. She felt terrible about what she'd done. She'd pay it all back.

By now, I was just a little suspicious of S. A little. It was a pretty good crying scene, but I wasn't completely moved. I was, in fact, still pretty furious. She got no, "Hey, we all make mistakes" platitudes from me. The only thing I agreed to was that I wouldn't press criminal charges if she made good on the money.

I returned home, called my attorney and told him about the lunch. He immediately prepared a payment schedule. S. signed it.

And of course, two months later, I still hadn't seen a dime.

I called my attorney. Where did we go from here? Well, he hit me with a bombshell: He was retiring. At the ripe of old age of 41, he'd made a bundle and wanted to go off and spend time with his family. But he had a brother, Bob, who was also an attorney; Bob even wanted to learn screenwriting, and Howard figured Bob would cut me a deal on lawsuit fees if I taught him screenwriting.

Strangely enough, that worked out just fine. Bob wasn't quite as high-powered as his bro, but I really did teach him screenwriting in exchange for his fees, and he did a good job. "Do you want to press criminal charges?," he asked at our first meeting.

"Will that affect her ability to make money and pay me back?," I asked.

"Probably," Bob answered.

So I decided not to press charges. To this day, I'm not sure if S. knows how lucky she was.

At least we were able to put her out of business as an agent – in California, agents have to post a $10,000 bond when they go into business, and Bob got us the bond money right off the bat. And I knew she wouldn't be taking advantage of any other trusting, naïve young writers.

Well…at least not as an agent. Because S. bounced right back as a fucking producer.

The good news is I finally got all the money back. Of course it took two years and lots of legal wrangling and liens and all kinds of un-fun stuff, but finally it was done.

After S., you can probably imagine that I wasn't exactly scrambling to find another agent. By then I was more interested in fiction anyway.

So, let's flash forward a few years now, and bring on Agent #2.

Sometime in the late '90s, a producer friend approached me about creating a television series for him. He'd just made a deal to obtain rights to the old '50s scifi movie *Teenagers from Outer Space*, and he thought he could do better shopping it as a series than doing a feature film. I hadn't seen the movie, and he cautioned me against watching it; all he wanted me to take was the title (to this day, I've still never seen *Teenagers from Outer Space*).

Buffy the Vampire Slayer had just started airing on the tube, and we all loved the show and agreed that our *Teenagers* should play like the science fiction version of *Buffy*, that it should be hip and funny and up-end a lot of genre tropes. This was right up my alley, so I created a show to match the title. My producer pal loved it and started showing it around.

He soon attracted the attention of a major agent who was the vice president of (at the time) the industry's third largest agency. Let's call him J. (uh-oh, another initial). J. suggested we attach a "show runner" to the project; a show runner is someone who has experiencing creating and producing other television series, preferably long-running hits. Attaching a good show runner can sell even a bad project.

J. got us a guy who was a legendary show runner. This guy had created at least three major hit series. He was known for his pitching skills; he could walk into any room and sell a series instantly to the toughest executive.

I was assigned to work through the concept a little more with Mr. Legend. When I arrived at his house for our first meeting, I was simultaneously intimidated and stunned – it was without question the biggest, wealthiest, most ostentatious house I'd ever been in, and it was gawdawful. Seriously...it looked like they'd hired Liberace on a bad acid trip to do the interior decorating. How could anyone with this much money have so little taste? The meetings were actually slightly uncomfortable for me because I couldn't quite shake the notion that I was sitting in a 19th-century Moroccan bordello.

But we finished polishing up the concept, and *Teenagers from Outer Space* was ready to hit the pitch trail. With J. and Mr. Legend attached, doors opened wide; our pitches took place at the top levels of every single major Hollywood network or studio. It was far and away the biggest project I'd ever been involved with. I was excited to be a part of it, if for no other reason than getting an inside look at how Hollywood worked at the apex.

So, you can probably imagine my surprise when I got my first look at Mr. Legend's mythological pitch skills, and thought, *You have GOT to be fucking kidding me.* I couldn't believe it. The guy read from a yellow legal pad in this booming, over-the-top voice, he periodically thrust his hands out excitedly, and he used phrases like "hot rod" (really? "Hot rod"? Isn't this the 1990s, not the 1950s?). I was aghast. No one would buy this ridiculous performance, surely.

But they did, of course. They stood in awe of Mr. Legend. They all grinned and nodded like monkeys on ecstasy. "Great job," they'd enthuse. And then of course, because they'd been thoroughly confused by the pitch (but wouldn't admit it), they'd turn to me and I'd fill in the gaps.

One day Mr. Legend couldn't make a pitch. We found out literally as we were walking across the parking lot heading for the offices where we were to have the meeting. "You're doing the pitch today," J. informed me, with no time whatsoever to prepare.

Okay, I thought, I can do this. It'll be fun.

And it was fun. I loved doing it (I remain one of the few writers I know who really likes to pitch; to me it's like telling a story around a campfire).

I knocked that fucking pitch out of the park. And I didn't use the word "hotrod" even once.

The executives were all grinning and nodding, but not like they did with Michael. "Wow," they said quietly. "That was a great pitch. We're going to think seriously about it."

By the time we were ten feet outside that office, J. was asking, "Who represents you?"

"Nobody right now," I told him.

A business card magically appeared in his hand. "Call me."

You bet your ass I called him. Yes, he wanted to represent me. I dumped my pile of unsold scripts on him. He'd be reading them and getting back to me.

By now, *Teenagers* was over. I still don't know what happened. We sat in the offices of TWO majors who said, "We'll get our bid in by the end of the day." I knew that if *Teenagers* did happen, it was likely I'd get shuffled off to the side, but I'd be set for life if I could retain even part of the "Created By" credit.

But somehow two bids didn't lead to a deal. My producer friend thought J. blew it.

Well, J. certainly had an interesting way of handling *me*. We had our first big meeting to discuss my various projects, but we never got very far because we were constantly interrupted by a neverending stream of J.'s other clients, most of whom were middle-aged male writers, just dropping by to say hi.

After the meeting, J. called with an odd suggestion: He wanted me to meet one of his other clients. He thought maybe we could work on something together. Sure, I said; I liked meeting new people.

My first warning should have been that the "meeting" was set for a swanky westside restaurant at 8 p.m. The other writer was one of the guys I'd seen in J.'s office. And it was soon quite apparent that this was not a meeting to discuss projects.

It was a date.

Yes, my new agent was pimping me out to his other clients for dates.

Needless to say, J. never did read any of my scripts or send me out on any meetings. I gave it six months, but at that point I just took my scripts back and walked out.

Agent #3 arrived a few years later. Judith was a woman who'd just left a successful production company because she wanted to be an agent and work with writers. We were introduced by mutual friends. Judith read a script and didn't just like it, she gave me good rewrite notes and a solid plan for shopping the script.

I did the rewrite. I came back two weeks later.

And found out Judith had just given up agenting to return to a better position at the successful production company.

Well, Judith's boss at the agency kept me as a client, and she was my film agent until she retired. In ten years of her repping me, she never sent me out for a single meeting. The last time she called me, she asked me if I wanted to move to New York and write soap operas. I politely declined.

About that time, I finished my first novel; it was a big, epic historical dark fantasy that had major series potential. I thought it was a slam dunk, especially given how many publishing credits I'd accrued with short fiction.

The first round of agent meetings and inquiries went nowhere. I came close a couple of times, but invariably there was that one guy in the office who didn't like my book.

Then I won my first Bram Stoker Award®. Maybe I could parlay that into a little agent action. Round #2 came and went without representation. My favorite rejection this time was, "I love you, I love your book, but I just sold something too close to it." Uhhh... isn't the most common piece of advice given to writers seeking an agent to find someone who's sold your kind of book? Yeah, well, just remember my sterling words of wisdom, gained from years of experience: It's all bullshit.

Fortunately I did finally acquire a literary agent, and if you haven't yet seen a Lisa Morton book on the *New York Times* Bestseller List...well, that's not Agent Bob's fault. It's a tough business, and timing matters more than talent.

I remain optimistic that someday – some impossible fucking day – my timing will finally be right. Or at least that I'll be smart enough to know instantly when I'm being dicked around.

Living in Toontown

I NEVER PLANNED ON BEING A HALLOWEEN EXPERT. Or a modelmaker. Or a cartoon writer. But somehow these things keep happening to me.

Back in the '90s, I had a friend named Eric who ran a graphic arts studio. Eric had read *Lightning Strikes* and thought it rocked. One day, Eric off-handedly asked if I'd mind if he showed *Lightning Strikes* to some guys he knew who were putting together a new children's cartoon show. Sure, I said…and thought nothing more about it. I used to hear this stuff all the time. It rarely led to anything.

One day, maybe six months later, I was working at my bookstore job when a FedEx package arrived for me. A big one. Odd; I wasn't expecting anything, and I didn't recognize the sender's name at all.

I opened it up, and tons of stuff poured out – scripts. Artwork. Booklets.

Contracts.

Wha-HUH?! Had they delivered this to the wrong address? This couldn't be for me, could it? Gifts didn't just fall out of the FedEx truck like this.

It took me a while to figure out what the hell this magical package was. I finally put it together: These were Eric's friends. They really were producing an animated series. It was an action show for girls (holy crap, right?). And they'd absolutely freaked out over *Lightning Strikes*, enough to not just make me an instant offer, but to actually try to woo me.

Well, it didn't take much wooing. Their show was incredible. Superheroes for girls! I was perfect for this. I'd even had a little experience with animation writing, when I'd written the script that Agent S. had taken her 100% commission on.

I went over everything they'd sent me (really, it was hundreds of pages of material), and loved it all. They'd already created the show's basic concept and the characters, and they'd put a lot of work into designs and concept art. It was all gorgeous.

The show was called *Sky Dancers*. If that's setting off an alarm bell somewhere in the back of your head and you're not sure why…read on.

The main producer was a guy named Anthony Gentile. We started talking a lot on the phone about *Sky Dancers*. I would be helping to refine the show's "Bible" (a basic guide to the show's concept, characters, and style), and would be working with Anthony and the show's other producers to craft the pilot script. Anthony was a fantastic guy who had actually written horror in the past (you can still find his novel *The Judas Seed* in used bookstores). I never did get to meet him in the flesh, but always enjoyed the phone conferences and letters.

Anthony ran Abrams/Gentile Entertainment with his brothers and an attorney named Marty Abrams. They'd really started as a company dedicated to toy design; they'd made waves with the Nintendo Power Glove. *Sky Dancers* had started as a toy; the series came after, and mainly existed as a way to promote the toys (which doesn't mean the Gentiles didn't take the show seriously – we all did). The Sky Dancer toys were cool as hell, and were really a whole new type of toy. They were little winged dolls mounted on bases that would spin and shoot off into the air when a string in the base was yanked. They flew up into the air about 30 feet, and then executed pretty little spins as their wings unfolded and they sailed slowly back down to earth.

I loved working on *Sky Dancers*. The toys were selling well, and the series was drawing good ratings. I started writing a lot of the shows, making nice money on every script I turned in. Because these things were short, I could (don't tell the Gentiles this!) actually write one in a night. Rewrites were often much harder than the first draft, because I'd receive two sets of notes – one from Anthony, and one from the French company Gaumont that was co-producing the show – and the notes would often be completely contradictory. But everyone was willing to talk stuff out, and we were all totally chuffed on the notion that we were creating positive, strong, smart role models for little girls. It didn't hurt that I was paying off my credit cards in the process.

With the success of *Sky Dancers*, Abrams/Gentile decided to launch a line of similar dolls for boys, and *Dragon Flyz* was born. I was too busy with *Sky Dancers* to participate much in the creation of *Dragon Flyz*, but I got to write four episodes of the show, including one that scored especially high in the ratings. I was now a staff writer on two popular syndicated kids' shows. My world was fiiiiine.

Until the day when some kid shot a Sky Dancer off and put out an eye.

Within days both the Sky Dancers and Dragon Flyz toys were the subjects of a nationwide recall. And of course that meant the series were over. A number of episodes I'd scripted of both shows had been completed when the plugs were abruptly pulled; I've never seen them, although I've heard they aired in Europe.

Fortunately the Gentiles were down but not out; they were soon back with a new toy and a new show. *Van-pires* was a neat new twist on Transformers: The central idea was that a meteor had hit a car wrecking yard and brought some of the old vehicles to life as "Van-pires", fiendish metallic creatures that roamed the roads at night in search of fuel; standing against them are four kids who've also been altered by the meteor and given the ability to change into superpowered automobiles. The Van-pires toys had already been designed and a major toy manufacturer had signed on to produce them. And the series would be a groundbreaker, because it was going to combine live-action and computer animation, which at the time was still in its infancy.

If anything, *Van-pires* was even more fun than *Sky Dancers* and *Dragon Flyz*. Although the show was heavy on the bad jokes (example: One of the bad guys was a talking toilet named "Flush"), the Gentiles weren't afraid to go dark on it, and rock music was also a big part of it (the show, in fact, was scored by John Entwistle of The Who – I mean, come ON, how cool is THAT?!). I had a big hand in creating the show, and had my pick of scripts to develop from concept to finished product. The show was an almost immediate hit, and became the #1 syndicated show for boys. Gaumont wasn't involved this time around and that made for easy rewrites; the Gentiles and I were all in synch.

(Side note: In 1999, I attended a vampire conference that was held in honor of the centennial of Dracula. I was assigned to appear on a panel about vampires in media, and at some point in the panel I mentioned *Van-pires*, which I was working on at the time. The audience loved it – but not so much one of my fellow panelists, a highly regarded non-fiction writer who proceeded to mock *Van-pires* in a less than amusing way. This same writer ended up stalking angrily off the panel for some other reason, and I've never forgiven him for his not-so-gentle mocking. Sorry, I shouldn't even have brought it up because now you're dying to know who it is, and I have other reasons for not telling you that. Buy me a drink sometime at a convention and maybe I'll tell you.)

And then – because, of course, with me, something always goes wrong – something went wrong. The toy manufacturer had just suddenly decided that it couldn't produce the toys after all. I never quite knew why.

All I know is that *Van-pires* had received a stake through the heart.

That was kind of it for the Gentiles, and who could blame them? There was talk of one more show that would have been the most amazing yet, because it would have been for adults: An animation series based on the Hammer horror films. The Gentiles had worked out a deal to acquire animation rights to the Hammer library, and of course I would be one of the principal writers, because there was no idea in history that was more perfect for me. Anthony loved the Hammer films as I did, and we started having phone conversations in which we divvied up the classic titles: "I want *Plague of the Zombies!*" "No way – I'm taking *Plague of the Zombies!*" "Okay, but I get *The Devil Rides Out*, then!"

Then something happened with the deal. It turned out they didn't have the rights to use the individual film plots or titles, only the Hammer name. No problem; we started creating plots that could have been Hammer films, but weren't.

Somehow it just never happened. The calls petered out. It's now been years since I've heard from the Gentiles. I still miss writing for them.

It was the best job I ever had.

I had one other kids' writing job that likewise came barreling at me from out of nowhere one day: My *Adventures in Dinosaur City* co-writer Wili Baronet and her new husband Mark Israel had just signed a deal to provide a daily show for Disney called *Toontown Kids*. The show would essentially consist of short live-action segments following two personable young hosts, Trevor and Liza, as they had adventures around Disneyland; the live-action segments wrapped around classic Disney cartoons. Mark would be doing the lion's share of the writing, but they needed 65 shows quickly, so I was brought in to take up the slack.

The best thing about *Toontown Kids* (aside from the checks, that is) is that I got some pretty great VIP access to Disneyland. I was given a copy of the official employee handbook, which was packed full of amazing facts, and taken behind the scenes. The show was designed to incorporate all kinds of Disneyland trivia, so if I had questions about some aspect of the park, I only had to pick up the phone.

The FCC ended up putting a damper on the heavy Disneyland aspects, saying that *Toontown Kids* couldn't play as little more than a commercial for the park, so we had to revamp our thinking a little under halfway through.

The other good part of *Toontown Kids* was my pretend office. While I was working on the show, I was also employed full-time as a bookseller. I refused to quit my bookseller job, naturally, even though Mark and Wili thought I should have an office at Disney, so everything would look kosher. We finally worked out a compromise: I would have a pretend office at Disney. I had a desk and chair and computer and piles of paper and a receptionist who was instructed to inform anyone who ever asked that I was out of the office for a while. I don't know if anyone ever did ask, but I found the idea very amusing.

Toontown Kids was my swan song to kids' shows. My film agent handled a lot of animation writers, and I tried to get in on other shows, but…well, if you've read my section on agents, you know that didn't work, even though I wrote new sample scripts for her to shop and even joined the Writers Guild's Animation Caucus for a while. Too bad, because I really enjoyed that part of my writing life.

Sky Dancers lives!

Roberta Lannes and I from a photo session for a 1996 horror writers' calendar (I believe the photo is by Nick Bougas)

Amanda Foubister, Mandy Slater, Stephen Jones and Dennis Etchison at the Iliad Bookshop

Why Weed and Filmmaking Don't Go Together Like Chocolate and Peanut Butter

AT SOME POINT IN THE EARLY '90S, an actor friend introduced me to two young filmmakers who wanted to make horror movies. These guys had already made some ultra-ultra-low-budget science fiction/action features, but horror was their first love.

We're going to call these guys Mutt and Jeff. Jeff was a tall, good-looking guy with tons of manic energy; Mutt was short, quiet, and laid back. They were sharing an apartment in the Hollywood hills that they'd also partly converted into a tiny film studio. The living room was barren of furniture, they'd painted one entire wall black, and set up the front end of an old car there so they could grab driving close-ups.

These guys tickled me, plus they were obviously committed; you meet a lot of people in Hollywood who jabber on endlessly about making movies, but never actually do it. Mutt and Jeff had done it, were doing it now, and wanted to do it forever. They had a lot of good ideas and interesting resources, so I said yes, I'd write a script for them.

We started talking about what they wanted. They wanted to do something with horror and with action, they had a specific location, and they even had a car they wanted to use. No problem; I could mix and match horror, action, road trip and science fiction movies, all in a desolate locale.

Oh, one other thing: They wanted to star in it.

Granted, that should have sent me running...but I liked the idea. Jeff had shown me some of his earlier movies that he'd acted in, and he was actually pretty good. He and Mutt together already made me laugh, so I imagined that tossing them some clever Lisa Morton dialogue might be the acme of comedy. It'd be a horror/action/road trip/science fiction/comedy.

I wrote the script. I wrote it very specifically with them in mind for the leads. The script turned out great. It was that odd mishmash I described above, but somehow it worked.

Mutt and Jeff loved it, too. They immediately started making plans on what they were going to do with it. And first up was how they were going to finance it:

They were going to grow and sell their own pot.

When they told me this, I thought they were joking...until they showed me the seven plants growing in a nice little hydroponic setup in the hallway closet. They figured they could get $50,000 out of the harvest. Enough to shoot the movie on, in other words.

After that, I lost touch with them for a while. I figured the plants were still maturing.

Then, probably six months later, Jeff reappeared. With quite a story.

He and Mutt had suffered a bad split. Mutt had moved out of the Hollywood apartment, and taken the plants with him. Jeff had spent a while tracking him down, but he finally did: Mutt was now sharing a house in the Valley. Jeff climbed the fence late one night, broke into the house, and stole the plants back.

I probably don't have to tell you the rest of this story...

Jeff pretty much smoked up the movie's budget. He sold just enough to live on, but that was it.

I never saw Mutt again, but I've heard from Jeff a few times over the years. The last time I talked to him, he'd called me late one night and said he was living back east somewhere, and that he'd called just to prove to his girlfriend that he actually knew a real writer. I think they'd seen *Tornado Warning* or something on television.

I always liked Mutt and Jeff, and I was saddened to realize that they never got to live their movie-making dreams...like the thousands of others who leave this town, broke and broken, every year.

I hope the grass was at least good.

My wet-suited, seventy-ish dad digging out abalones from a tide pool in Northern California

Me facing out *Hell Manor* in the Iliad Bookshop

Little Stories

AFTER READING ABOUT MY ENCOUNTERS with thieving agents, dopers, scissors-wielding madmen, and eye-gouging toys, you can probably understand when I say that I was ready to leave screenwriting and theater behind, at least for a while. Which left only one thing…

Back in the early '80s, I met a writer named Dennis Etchison through Ray Bradbury. Dennis was teaching a writing course at UCLA, and Ray was a guest speaker one night (and, if you can believe it, I drove them both to UCLA – I think I've never driven as carefully as I did that night). I knew nothing about Dennis or his work, but I was impressed by things he said in the class and his obvious intelligence, so I picked up his short story collection *The Dark Country* and started to read.

Pause here to insert another life-changing experience.

Obviously I grew up loving horror, but throughout most of the '70s I'd fed on a steady diet of science fiction. Aside from bestselling novels (Blatty, King, Tryon), I for some reason read very little horror in that decade, and almost no short fiction. Part of it, I think, was that horror still seemed stuck in the past somehow. Even a book like *Salem's Lot* – which remains my favorite Stephen King novel – dealt with vampires, and in the sort of small town suburbia I had no relation to whatsoever.

But Etchison…my God, these stories were like someone had stepped into the back of my brain and started pulling out the dark bits and forcing me to look. It didn't hurt, of course, that most of Dennis's work is set in the Southern California I know so well – the canyons, the hills, the flatlands, the odd parts of the Valley; but these stories were also completely contemporary. There wasn't a vampire or Gothic flourish to be found. These stories dealt with fears I could completely relate to, fears of class differences and medical science and loss and mistakes and urban living.

By the time I'd finished *The Dark Country*, I knew I could – and would – write horror fiction. These were the sorts of stories that had been floating in my subconscious for years, but somehow I'd never thought about telling them like this.

Well, it took me a few years to put away my screenwriting toys and come to my fiction senses. After *Adventures in Dinosaur City*, as I became aware of the new notion that I didn't relish life as a movie flunkie, I started to write these stories at last. They spilled out quickly; I wrote (I think) about six right off the bat.

Of course I had no idea what I was doing. This, mind you, was back in the days before the internet; there were no easy ways to access information on formatting or markets. I learned how to format from looking at some copies of Harlan Ellison manuscripts that my local used bookstore was selling (and I still got it wrong – one of my first submissions was to Ellen Datlow, who politely informed me that one didn't staple manuscripts). So I typed up those first half-dozen or so pieces on my electric typewriter and then shoved them in a notebook, having absolutely no idea of what to do with them.

Fate smiled on me. Not long after, I met Roberta Lannes, when Rocky Heck and I staged a reading of her one-act play *Marionette*. Roberta and I became friends, and eventually I worked up the nerve to ask Roberta if she'd look at the stories. She did. She read them.

And she told she thought they were almost all instantly publishable.

So...what should I do next, I asked her. Her answer: Come with me to the World Fantasy Convention. It was coming up in Minneapolis, and Roberta needed a roomie. It was the convention for anyone looking to break into horror writing (this was before the World Horror Convention even existed, so there was more emphasis on horror at World Fantasy Conventions). I said yes.

It was the smartest thing I ever did.

We'd barely arrived at the Minneapolis hotel before Roberta and Dennis whisked me off to the first party and started introducing me around. Dennis trotted me up to everybody and announced, "This is Lisa – she wrote *Meet the Hollowheads!*" Now, I was thinking, *God, Dennis, nobody has seen that thing*...except that everybody at World Fantasy had not only seen it, they effin' loved it. Kim Newman even told me he'd been at a London film festival where it had won the top prize, something I'd never known before.

There were three highlights of that first convention for me:

Highlight #1: At a party on the first night, a very nice man descended on me when he found out I'd written *Hollowheads*. This guy practically worshiped the movie. He quoted lines to me that I'd written. I kept thinking he looked vaguely familiar, so I finally asked him what he did. "Oh, I just work on a little local television show shot here in Minneapolis," he answered. I asked him what it was called.

"*Mystery Science Theater 3000.*"

Then I recognized him instantly – he was Trace Beaulieu, one of the stars and creators of MST3K, which of course I loved. I told him they should do *Hollowheads*. "Oh, no," he said, in all seriousness, "it's too good. We really only do bad movies." Wow, this convention was GREAT!

Highlight #2: Driving Dennis and his wife Kris to the massive Mall of America in my rental car. Dennis was currently brooding about a feud with Harlan Ellison, and was offering to throw five of his stories in a wrestling ring with five of Ellison's stories. At the Mall, Dennis was doing a signing in a chain bookstore with three other authors – Steve and Melanie Tem, and Poppy Z. Brite. Nobody showed up for the signing. The four authors got so bored they proceeded to read their stories to each other. It was the first time I'd heard anything of Poppy's work, and I was an instant fan.

Highlight #3: Stephen Jones, an editor so renowned that even I, in my newbie horror lover state, knew his name, was also a *Hollowheads* fan and said he'd read anything I sent him.

He turned down the first story I sent. But he bought the second one.

It was a short story adaptation of my play *Sane Reaction*, and it appeared in the 1994 anthology *Dark Voices 6*, which Steve co-edited with David Sutton. Steve also bought the next story I sent him ("Poppi's Monster", for *The Mammoth Book of Frankenstein*), and he remains the editor who I've worked with the most, a fact for which I count myself very, very lucky indeed.

The title of this essay derives from an experience I had not long after I'd sold those first two stories to Steve. I'd sold a few other things as well, and one day I ran into an actress I'd worked with in my theater company First Stage Alert. She was one of those types that just exudes a sort of fake, passive-aggressive over-the-top sunniness. She asked what I'd been up to since I'd left theater. I told her about the short fiction sales. "Well," she said, with a dazzling, ear-to-ear grin, "that's great about your little stories!"

Sure, I wanted to slug that condescending smile off her pretty face, but I didn't, because I was so damn proud of those stories that her bullshit didn't much matter.

That first time you see a book with your work in it is always special for any writer, but it had an extra meaning for me: I looked at that copy of *Dark Voices 6* (it was a mass market paperback), and I saw my story in there, and I thought: *This is right. This is where I belong. Not in Hollywood, and not on stage.* This, the printed page, this was where I fit.

Me and my little stories.

And that fortunately, hasn't changed, more than twenty years later.

Some Stories Behind Stories

EVERY WRITER HAS GOTTEN THE DREADED, "Where do you get your ideas?" question (although with us horror writers, it might be couched in terms more along the lines of, "What happened to you as a child that you think this stuff up now?" See the first essay in this book for the answer to that.)

As with any writer, a fair amount of my work is inspired by something that's happened in everyday life. Sometimes the stories behind the stories are pretty doggone crazy unto themselves, so I thought I'd share five of my favorites right here.

"Black Mill Cove" (originally appeared in *Dark Delicacies*)
WHAT THE STORY IS ABOUT: Jim, a lone hunter looking for abalone in an isolated Northern California tide pool, finds a serial killer stashing body parts instead.

WHAT INSPIRED IT: I was once at a party where a young man approached me who'd just read this story; he told me he loved it, but thought the first half - which describes the solitary hunter hiking several miles over rough terrain and then crawling 30 feet down a sheer cliff to totter precariously along slippery tide pools all in pre-dawn darkness - was somewhat unbelievable. I, of course, burst into laughter and told him I'd actually done exactly that.

A few years ago, I went up north to visit my dad. It was supposed to be a quick visit...but on the drive up my car's transmission went to Toyota Heaven, so I was stuck with Pop for a few extra days while the car had a new transmission put in. Pop had an abalone excursion planned, so I was along for the ride.

Dad lived in San Jose, so step one was a two-hour drive north, in Dad's huge, creaking old motor-home, past San Francisco and through Marin County, to wind along the narrow, two-lane, cliff-hugging Highway One for the last forty minutes, convinced that we were about to plunge to our deaths in the Pacific Ocean any second. Finally we reached Dad's preferred campground, pulled in...and this was about the time that I was informed that low-tide was at 6 a.m., so we had to leave at 4:30 in the morning. This is normal for my dad. It's anathema for me.

But I got up with Dad, who wore a wetsuit (I didn't) as we left my sleeping stepmother in the motor-home and started hiking. His special super-secret cove was a mile or so off. The terrain was full of thistles and critters and pot-holes that were easy to miss in the tiny beam from the flashlight. Oh, yeah - and more sheer drops. Seriously, the cliff edge would suddenly appear three inches to my left and I'd veer to the right just in time. I probably don't need to add that we were the only people out there at this insane time of night.

Finally Pop spotted his special bush. Uhhh...WHAT?! I'm not kidding. His special shrub was the only way he could locate the narrow ravine that led down to his abalone-packed cove. "So, how do we get down?", I asked. Silly of me, I know.

"Just climb down. It's not that far," Dad said, as he lowered himself past the bush and into the ravine.

The ravine petered out just a few feet down, and the rest was pretty much clinging on for dear life to rough stone - all done, mind you, in complete darkness, because it took two hands to climb down.

Somehow I made it to the bottom intact. Now we walked past tide-pools and over slippery kelp to an outcropping where I perched as Pop waded out to just where the ocean started in earnest.

For the first hour, of course, there wasn't much to see. I had my camera with me, but there was no light. Finally the sun rose, the fog (oh, did I forget to mention that, too?) burned off fairly quickly, and by around 7:30 the surroundings actually became interesting. I've always been a fan of marine life and tide-pools, thanks to a sixth grade teacher I had who took us on trips to the San Diego tide-pools and kept a salt-water aquarium in the classroom. These pools were full of beautiful sea life - colorful starfish and sea urchins and anemones - and I was happy to occupy myself snapping away. At one point I looked up and saw something that made my heart leap into my throat: Dad was in the ocean proper now, only his head poking up out of the water - and some sort of large creature was circling around him in the water. Shark! of course popped into my head immediately...and then a sleek, pretty little head broke the surface, and I realized it was a playful sea otter.

By this time the tide was coming back in, which was resulting in lots of sea spray as the waves crashed up against the rocks...sea spray that was going right into my eyes. Soon they were so swollen and painful I couldn't even take pictures any longer; I could only sit back against the cliff with my eyes closed and tears streaming down my cheeks.

Finally, around 10 a.m., Dad had his limit (three abalone), and we could leave. Now I had the joy of climbing back up that cliff with my eyes in agony. Somehow I managed it. We trudged back to the motor-home, and the worst of the ordeal was over.

I do have to admit the abalone for lunch that day was damned tasty.

"Blind-stamped" (originally appeared in *Shelf Life: Fantastic Stories Celebrating Bookstores*)

WHAT THE STORY IS ABOUT: A young man who lives in the used bookstore he's recently opened finds out that his space is haunted after he buys a library from a man who was recently deceased.

WHAT INSPIRED IT: In 1991, at the end of the year when I was going stir-crazy trying to live as a full-time writer, I took a job at a local used bookstore, the Iliad Bookshop, to ground myself again. Twenty years later, the store moved, but I moved with it. Taking that job was a good decision.

When I first started working at the store, it'd been open for only about four years. The owner, Dan Weinstein, still lived in the store; in a back room, sealed away from the store, Dan had a little loft where he slept with a full bath below. There was even a buzzer at the front of the store that I could press to call for Dan if I really needed him. He likes to stay up late and sleep in late, so I avoided using that buzzer as much as possible until he was wide awake.

We used to have a regular customer named Rick. Rick was a man in late middle age who was a serious bibliophile. He spent a lot of money with us, and I guessed that he was unmarried; he was a nice enough fellow, but seemed to prefer the company of books to humans.

Rick suddenly stopped showing up. Almost a year went by before we saw him again. The intervening year had not been kind to Rick: He was gaunt, sickly, and was bringing in books to sell. He had cancer.

Rick continued to sell us books for a few months, then we stopped seeing him altogether. I can only assume he finally succumbed to the cancer. We used to wonder if we'd get a call asking us to appraise his collection, but we never did. A lot of it had been sold back to us, but not all. I still wonder what happened to the rest.

The best praise I got on this story came from *Shelf Life* editor Greg Ketter, who told me he totally identified with it, having apparently lived in his store for a while as well. That made me very happy.

"Face Out" (originally appeared in *Help! Wanted: Tales of On-the-Job Terror*)

WHAT THE STORY IS ABOUT: Megan, who manages a chain bookstore and is unhappy with policies that increasingly emphasize books as mere products, is suddenly surrounded by living books that will do anything to protect themselves...and her.

WHAT INSPIRED IT: Back in the mid-'80s, in between special effects gigs, I managed a Waldenbooks for a few years (I've worked in bookstores since I was 14, when my mom gave me a summer job in the college bookstore she managed and paid me off in used textbooks and art supplies). I managed a small Waldenbooks in the Westchester suburb of L.A. near LAX; we weren't in a mall, and had a lovely regular clientele of neighborhood folks, many of whom we knew by both first name and reading preference. My staff prided themselves on customer service, and we were one of the best performing stores in the chain for our size.

None of which mattered to upper management. Our district manager was an incredibly bland guy who was so strictly by-the-book that it was ridiculous. We had a store that faced onto a parking lot and was directly in the flight path of one of the world's busiest airports, so a lot of dirt got tracked in. Our district manager constantly compared our cleanliness standards to mall stores. "Give me a budget for cleaning and it won't be a problem," I'd say. "Mall stores have mall employees who clean up around storefronts," I'd add.

"You need to spend more time on cleaning," he'd say.

"But we're making a lot of money putting that time into customer service."

I might as well have been talking to a brick wall. It was pointless.

There was a regional manager over the district manager's head, and he often praised our store. But again…nothing seemed to make sense to the district manager.

The final straw for me came on the day they held a management seminar for all the Southern California Waldenbooks managers. We all arrived at the hotel conference room in Orange County bright and early. We feasted on free Danish, then sat down to get the pep talk.

And here's what they told us: "There should be no difference between selling a book and a bar of soap. And if you're in this because you love books…get out."

I didn't even stay for the whole seminar. I left at the lunch break. I even stole another Danish on my way out as a final act of rebellion. It didn't matter to me that I had absolutely no idea what I'd do or where I'd go. I only knew then what I've known my entire life: Books aren't bars of soap. Bars of soap serve one purpose: To get you clean. Books are the heart and soul of a culture. They can entertain, enlighten, educate, arouse, and even change a life. They are sacred objects to me.

I got lucky and found a secretarial position right away. I wrote Waldenbooks a scathing letter on my way out. My entire staff followed me out the door (although I begged them not to). And as for Waldenbooks...well, considering that they were acquired by K-Mart shortly after I left, and fell to ruin soon thereafter, I hope that somewhere along the line, they also realized that a book was not a bar of soap.

Nah...they probably blamed their failure on managers who didn't meet cleanliness standards.

"Golden Eyes" (originally appeared in *Horror Library Volume 3*)

WHAT THE STORY IS ABOUT: An upscale couple living in a Los Angeles canyon find their home increasingly invaded by a variety of local wild animals...and realize this is the beginning of a war.

WHAT INSPIRED IT: Back in the mid-'90s, I was living in the flatlands of the San Fernando Valley (where I still live), reasonably far away from anything that could even remotely be construed as wilderness...and yet for about a year I kept encountering animals that had no right being in the middle of suburbia.

It started simply, with the occasional possum or squirrel. Then it progressed to coyotes. There are a lot of coyotes around L.A.; it's hardly unusual to round a curve in a canyon road at night and see their eyes glinting in your headlights. But when you start meeting up with packs of them...it gets a little unnerving.

Then there was the hawk.

One morning I opened the Iliad Bookshop as always. I'd arrived a little early, because one of my co-workers, who lived right behind the store, was on vacation and I was taking care of his cats. I opened the door to his little duplex apartment, and the male cat, Torquemada, trotted out into the fenced-in yard between the apartments and the store. I followed Torque out...

And there, sitting on a small fence no more than thirty feet away, was the biggest damned hawk I've ever seen.

Seriously, this thing was huge. It was nearly three feet tall as it sat there, with those huge curving talons gripping the wooden fence, and that immense, lethal-looking beak...

...and of course it was staring at the cat. Who was staring at it. While he ran towards it.

I was speechless for a second. I was overcome with visions of trying to explain to my returned co-worker how the world's biggest fucking hawk had carried his cat away.

Finally I found my voice. "TORQUE!" I shouted.

That did it, thank God. The hawk took off. Torque froze, looking up in disappointment as that monster flapped away, never realizing how close he'd been to ending up as Filet O' Torquemada.

The final weird animal sighting was late one night, as I was returning home from something or other. A block from my apartment my headlights caught some motion in the gutter. As I neared, I actually slowed down and stopped, staring in disbelief.

It was a family of raccoons. Four of them.

I had friends living in the Hollywood hills who'd reported raccoons raiding their trash (they also had the occasional skunk visit; I'd had the misfortune of dog-sitting once when the dog had been sprayed, and I'd learned the finer points of removing skunk smell from dog fur with tomato juice), but I'd never seen them in my area, and certainly not a family. Someone told me later that they were probably using the sewer drains to move around in.

The strange animal sightings have died down recently, but I

figure that's probably just because they're moving more covertly these days while they plot their takeover.

"The Urban Legend"/"San Diablo" (originally appeared in *Monsters of L.A.* and *Allen K.'s Inhuman Magazine #5*)

WHAT THE STORIES ARE ABOUT: Young women discover that Los Angeles is actually home to a race of lizard people who live beneath the city streets.

WHAT INSPIRED IT: About 2002, I was researching *The Halloween Encyclopedia* and I used the Los Angeles Public Library's website a lot. One day I noticed a tiny line of print buried down at the bottom of the main page, something about library trivia and the Lizard People who lived beneath the downtown library. There was a link to a page with a few, all-too-brief sentences (this page is long gone now, so don't look for it).

This, needless to say, piqued my interest bigtime. I love L.A. folklore, and there's more of it around than most people know. A few searches for the Lizard People online turned up one of the most intriguing stories in Southern California's history: In the 1930s, an entrepreneur named G. Warren Shufelt filed a patent on a device that he claimed could find nearly anything via the use of "radio waves". Shufelt came to the city of Los Angeles and convinced them that his invention had found gold beneath the city's streets. Amazingly enough, the city gave Shufelt permission to drill, as long as he shared the gold with the city.

Shufelt started drilling, and the story got stranger. Shufelt soon acquired a map given to him supposedly by a Hopi Indian chief; the map, which outlined 30 miles worth of tunnels beneath L.A., came with the legend of a race of Lizard People who had built the tunnels and lined them with gold.

The more I researched this thing (and yes, I confess it became a minor obsession), the stranger it got. At some point Shufelt just completely vanished. Did the Lizard People claim him? Or did the retired army officer he'd gotten to bankroll his project finally catch on and send a posse after him? Or was the truth far more mundane - that Shufelt was just one more of those who left L.A., his dreams shattered into fool's gold?

In any case, I've followed the story of Shufelt and the Lizard People for years, and it led to other interesting stories of local folklore as well - one, the tale of the catwoman "La Japonesa", wound up as the "Cat People" story in my collection *Monsters of L.A.*, while another, that of the scorned young woman who cursed Los Feliz in 1863, became the basis for my novel *Malediction*. The Lizard People first appeared in my first novel, *Netherworld*, then found their way into the "Urban Legend" novelette from *Monsters of L.A.* and the short story "San Diablo".

I promise I'll stop writing about the Lizard People. At least for a while.

Tsui Hark in his office

A typical street in Hong Kong. I know you'd rather see a photo of Brigitte Lin Ching-hsia, but I managed to leave Hong Kong without one (*sigh*)

Go East, Young Woman

I AM OBSESSED WITH ASIAN CINEMA.

To many of you, this is no surprise. Maybe you've read my column "The East is Red" in one of its several incarnations. Maybe you know that my first book was called *The Cinema of Tsui Hark*. Maybe you even know me, and have heard me wax rhapsodic over some movie from Hong Kong or South Korea or Japan.

This obsession started – as it did with many of us Asian cinephiles – with one of those passed-around bootleg tapes. This was back in the day before DVDs, and stuff from across the Pacific was hard to get and shared like expensive booze. A friend gave me a copy of *The Killer* with instructions to watch it and return it in 24 hours. I did. And he was right – it blew me away. What was this editing style about? Check out those camera moves. The colors were saturated to the point of being eyeball-searing. And who WAS that insanely charismatic leading man?

The Killer was a gateway drug for a lot of us. I definitely wanted more. Not long after, a local art-house theater started running double features of recent Hong Kong movies. Coming up next, something called *Naked Killer* and another called *Green Snake*. The buzz on *Naked Killer* was pretty good. I didn't know the other one, but figured what the hell.

Naked Killer was first…and I didn't like it all, even though the audience ate up its combination of lurid, sensationalized sex and violence. It was *The Killer* with more speed and less art, and it just didn't work for me. Hmmm...maybe *The Killer* had been an anomaly...

Then the second one came on – *Green Snake*. The audience didn't care for this. They got restless. They started to leave. It didn't have the high adrenaline absurdity of *Naked Killer*.

I, on the other hand, thought (and still do) that it was the most swooningly beautiful film I'd ever seen. Its story of two snakes who become human women was erotic without being overtly sexualized, drenched in glorious deep greens and blues, scored like some insane cross between Indian ragas and Chinese opera, and it starred two of the most astonishing actresses I'd ever seen.

Well, a week later came another double feature, and this time the one I was smitten by was *The East is Red*, the third film in a trilogy. Soon thereafter, I saw that movie's immediate predecessor, *Swordsman 2*, which had the over-amped frenzy of *Naked Killer*, but it worked brilliantly in this movie, thanks in no small part to the performances (Jet Li and Brigitte Lin).

Who were the people making these films? I had to know.

Information was hard to come by. There were few websites on these films, no books except a few that were essentially fan publications, no DVDs with supplementary materials, and the oddball overseas magazine here and there.

I started to piece it together, and you can imagine my astonishment when I discovered that *The Killer, Green Snake, The East is Red*, and *Swordsman II* (in addition to a few others I'd seen by then, like *A Better Tomorrow* and *Once Upon a Time in China* and *A Chinese Ghost Story*) all had one name in common: Tsui Hark.

Who was this demented genius?

I began tracking down every iota of information I could. Because it was so hard to come by, I figured maybe others might also be looking for the same data and I could share. I created a website dedicated to Tsui Hark's works. I included reviews, frame captures, information on where to find these films, all the biographical tidbits I'd gathered.

Somewhere along the line – I don't remember the exact sequence of events now – Tsui Hark found out about the website. His wife, the acclaimed producer Nansun Shi, wrote me. My God – this was like touching God. He was global cinema's mad genius, and I had access to him.

I started thinking about a book. I knew it was kind of a niche thing, something unlikely to interest New York publishers, but I'd always liked the film books produced by McFarland, so I shot off a proposal to them. They said "yes" almost instantly.

Could I interview Tsui for the book, I begged Nansun?

Sure, she answered…but wouldn't it be best to do it in person, in Hong Kong?

Now, I'm not the world's most experienced traveler – in fact, at that point I'd never set foot off the North American continent – but there was no way I could turn that down. So plans were made, and soon I was jetting off to Hong Kong for a week with Tsui Hark.

I had no idea what to expect. I knew the city from the (by then) hundreds of Hong Kong films I'd devoured, but I also realized those were, of course, fiction. I had travel guides that warned me to expect the rudest city in the world. This was only a few years after the city had been handed over from Great Britain to China – would Americans still be welcome? And then there was Tsui – what would he be like? Would I have to work to get him to talk? Would he be open to a few more (ahem) probing questions? Would he get bored with me?

My first hint that the trip would go well was on the plane from

Seoul (where I'd transferred planes) to Hong Kong. I started chatting with a delightful young man who was seated next to me, and he was very impressed when he found out the purpose of my visit to Hong Kong. It turned out that his favorite movie was Tsui Hark's *The Lovers*. He told me all about how many times he'd seen it, and how it had brought him together with his girlfriend.

I got off the plane at the Hong Kong airport in the middle of the night, found the right bus over to the Kowloon side, arrived at my hotel an hour later, and settled in to battle jet lag. I had two days to explore Hong Kong on my own before I was set to meet Tsui.

Any reservations I might have had evaporated in about an hour of roaming the Tsim Sha Tsui district of Hong Kong. This really was the city of Hong Kong movies. It was fast, colorful, and exciting. And I could only assume that the travel writers who had called it the rudest city on earth had never been to Los Angeles, because everywhere I went, Hong Kong people were kind and helpful (Tsui would later tell me that was because I was a woman).

In two days, I conquered the subway system, bought enough movies to need a second backpack, ventured into the Temple Street night market (where you really could easily spot the Triad gangsters – I even bought a hilariously bad bootleg movie from one), sampled from Hong Kong's plentiful bakeries (yes, they love bakeries), and found a fantastic local health food restaurant where I could get superb, cheap meals. I even walked right by Chow Yun-fat – yes, that charismatic star of *The Killer* – coming out of the subways (and yes, I'm sure it was him, if for no other reason than the businessman in front of me who literally tripped over his own feet upon seeing Chow, who walked along with a duffel bag slung over one shoulder as if he was not the handsomest man alive).

Then it was time. The big day.

A subway and a taxi took me to the towering office complex which housed Film Workshop, Tsui's company. I arrived a few minutes before the appointed time, and waited near an editing station where an assistant was going over bits of footage from Tsui's latest film, an action thriller called *Time and Tide*. The footage looked spectacularly good.

Finally I was shown into the man's office. He was there. We chatted, then got down to business...

And I loved this guy.

He was everything I'd hoped for and more. If you've ever seen Tsui interviewed, maybe you have some idea of how this man's mind works. A simple question will lead him to spin off in a thousand directions, explore each of those, and then somehow bring it all back to a final, single answer, leaving you stunned and feeling like someone just exploded your brain with idea pills. He was amazing. He gave me material I never expected to get. We also started to discover things we had in common – we both loved the films of Japanese animation master Hayao Miyazaki, and we both liked graphic novels (Tsui's office was lined floor-to-ceiling with manga – "you should see the house," his wife later told me). But it was on the second day of our interview when I thought maybe I'd totally won him over. I'd just asked him about the use of contact lenses in The East is Red (lead actress Joey Wong is outfitted with blue contacts).

"You saw that?" he asked. "How?"

"I thought I noticed it in the theater, so I ran the tape back and forth a few times at home, just to be sure," I told him.

He eyed me with fresh appreciation and said, "Aaahhh...so you're a detail-oriented person."

You could also call me a perfectionist. Like...uh...Tsui Hark.

We had dim sum that day at a huge restaurant in the bottom of the tower. Tsui's doctor had recently placed him on some odd dietary restrictions, and he wasn't happy about that. In any case, we ate with two fellows he was working on a project with. Sadly neither one spoke English, so I couldn't engage them much, but one in particular was an interesting, very expressive fellow. It wasn't until years later that I finally put it together: He was director Herman Yau, who made the astonishing horror film *The Untold Story*, as well as a number of other fine Hong Kong films.

Tsui and I spent half of one day just kind of playing around. He was getting very interested in CGI at the time, and he showed me some of the programs he was working with. He told me how Hong Kong typewriters worked (there are over 800 characters in common usage in written Chinese, but they're all formed from the same 24 strokes), and gave me a demonstration. He gave me a stunning graphic novel he'd illustrated (he would have been a comics artist if film hadn't paid off), then really pulled out the stops and presented me with a gigantic, original pencil sketch from the novel.

"Tsui, it's beautiful, but...well...I don't know how I'll get it home," I told him. So he had it shipped to me, with a beautiful inscription (it still hangs on my bedroom wall).

But the best was yet to come.

"We are having a special dinner tonight to celebrate my friend James Wong," he told me. Wong was the composer of *Green Snake*'s delirious score, as well as the soundtracks for a number of other Tsui Hark movies. "He just finished a successful concert series. Why don't you join us?"

Wong was one of the Tsui collaborators I most wanted to meet. I knew this wouldn't exactly be an interview opportunity, but I was beyond thrilled.

We were joined by Nansun (whose dead-on impression of a bubble-headed Hollywood studio receptionist had me in stitches) and their friend Alex, who turned out to be Oliver Stone's producer (under the name "A. Kitman Ho"). We all piled into Tsui's SUV and headed across Hong Kong, taking the Cross Harbour Tunnel. Alex was particularly interested in what I thought of Tsui's use of women.

"He makes the most interesting use of women of any director in the world," I answered without a second thought. Tsui, who was driving, kind of smiled.

We arrived at a restaurant in Central and were shown to a private dining room. Tsui asked me to join him in a brandy, then he got a twinkle in his eye. "Oh, a few other people be joining us. You know Ti Lung?"

Okay, this would be like asking an American movie buff if they know Steve McQueen. Ti Lung was one of the biggest stars in Hong Kong during the '70s, when he was one of the leading martial arts actors for the Shaw Brothers, and Tsui had resurrected his career in 1986 to co-star in *A Better Tomorrow*.

"Uh, yeah – I know Ti Lung."

Then he dropped the real bombshell. "Oh, and…ah…Brigitte Lin."

I stared at him in disbelief for a minute. He was smirking. Was this a naughty little joke?

Thirty seconds later Brigitte Lin walked in.

Most westerners know Brigitte Lin Ching-hsia as the blonde from Wong Kar-wai's *Chungking Express*, but anyone who has seen *Swordsman 2* will never forget her brilliant, fierce performance as Asia the Invincible, a warrior who was castrated himself to achieve ultimate kung fu power and has become a beautiful woman in the process. Asia the Invincible could reduce opponents to puddles with just a glare, and now I was having dinner with her. "I'm sorry, my English not very good," she said.

"It's better than my Cantonese," I told her. Or at least I think I said that – this woman was so radiantly exquisite up close it was hard to not just stare, slack-jawed.

As she turned away from us, Tsui elbowed me and whispered, "That Brigitte Lin!"

I'm sure I would have howled if I wasn't still recovering from witnessing a goddess. "Yeah, I know," was all I could manage.

That dinner was magnificent. I sat wedged in between Tsui and Ti Lung. I teased Tsui about the fact that he spent half of dinner moving his fork around as if it were a mouse. I looked down at the tattoos poking out from under the cuff of Ti Lung's suit.

At this point, I confess that I'd seen very few of Ti Lung's classic martial arts films; I really knew him as the excellent older actor of dramas like *A Better Tomorrow*. A few years ago, a Hong Kong company called Celestial started releasing the entire Shaw Brothers library on DVDs and I finally got to see Ti Lung as a younger star – and he was dashing and sexy and handsome, and it's just as well that I hadn't seen those things yet, or I probably would have simply been overcome and passed out right there at the table.

And James Wong was a character-and-a-half. He and Tsui obviously had a very special relationship; Wong gesticulated wildly and leaned over the table as he talked about the joys and frustrations of working with Tsui.

And the food…oh my God. Course after course. Exquisite soufflés. Crab steamed in coconut milk. It was a completely lunatic amount of food. By about course number fourteen, I could barely lift my fork – and here were these Asians, some of whom were probably half my weight, still putting it away.

"Don't you like it?" Tsui asked.

"It's incredible, but…how can you keep eating?!"

"Chinese metabolism," he said. He was right.

Finally the food stopped coming, and the meal was over. My final special memory for the evening came courtesy of Ti, who – as we were waiting for cars to be brought around – gave me a warm smile and handshake, and told me he was very pleased to have met me. I think he actually meant it. He was an amazing man.

My time in Hong Kong was almost at an end, and it was just as well – I'd picked up something somewhere along the way, and by the time I flew home I had a 103-degree fever. I remember staggering through customs with all those movies I'd bought in Hong Kong, and just kind of collapsing in the car when Ricky picked me up. I could barely make it up the stairs at home.

But of course it was well worth it. Years later, I'd occasionally run into some Hong Kong movie fan I didn't know; we'd talk for a while, and then they'd suddenly say, "Wait – are you the American woman who had dinner with Brigitte Lin?" I still don't know how that got around.

My only regret is that I haven't stayed more in touch with Tsui and Nansun. I still don't really know how Tsui felt about the finished book. I do know that *Time and Tide* was excellent, then Tsui's career kind of flattened throughout the 2000s, but he came back with a vengeance in 2010 with the near-masterpiece *Detective Dee and the Mystery of the Phantom Flame* (for which he won the Hong Kong equivalent of the Directing Oscar).

And I also know that I owe the greatest night of my life to him. For that I will always be deeply grateful. Thank you, Tsui Hark.

Back in La-la Land

I SOMETIMES FEEL LIKE AL PACINO in *Godfather III* – every time I think I've escaped Hollywood, it pulls me back in.

After *Adventures in Dinosaur City*, that film's director Brett Thompson introduced me to a company he did frequent business with. Regent Entertainment made a lot of small feature films, both for television and for direct-to-DVD release; their one big theatrical success had been *Gods and Monsters*, the superlative James Whale biopic with Ian McKellen. When I first started working with them, they were just starting to move more into gay-themed entertainment; within a few years they would launch HereTV, a satellite channel specializing in LGBT movies and series, and they'd also later expand into other media. But when I started hanging out with them, they were making mainly non-gay-specific low-budget movies.

When Brett first brought me into Regent, they needed made-for-tv disaster movies. We pitched them a few things – tsunamis, earthquakes – but they finally went for one about tornados. They liked the story we'd built into the disaster, about an estranged father and daughter who are reunited in the face of catastrophe. We developed a few versions of the treatment, then were given the go-ahead to write the script.

Being a lifelong Californian, I of course knew virtually nothing about tornados, but endeavored to educate myself quickly (especially since our father in the script was a tornado expert). I learned that a lot of the commonly accepted safety practices during hurricanes were all wrong, so I thought perhaps I could make our script both entertaining and informative.

The script turned out pretty well. We had a couple of meetings with the director, Tibor Takacs, and worked out a polish. We had a few of the usual contradictory notes from various network and production company execs ("Add a younger sister/No, don't add a younger sister"), but managed to negotiate those slippery paths. Regent was very kind to Brett and I in the money department, and the movie finally went into production, with two fine actors – Gerald McRaney and Thea Gill – in the lead roles.

The movie shot in Canada, so I was never around the set…but lo and behold, who should walk into the Iliad Bookshop about three weeks after filming wrapped but Gerald McRaney. He was shopping with his wife, actress Delta Burke. He finally came up to buy some books, and I could contain myself no longer. "You're not going to believe this," I said, "but I wrote your last movie."

He stared for a second as if I was quite obviously insane, then I said, "You just finished *Tornado Warning*, right?"

He relaxed at that, and figured out I was for real. Then he kind of leaned forward and said, "Uhhh…they made some changes to the script." Amusingly enough, they'd taken all the stuff I'd inserted about proper tornado safety procedures and flipped it all back to the wrong way. Oh well.

The movie turned out well enough that the PAX cable channel decided to launch their 2002 fall season with it. The ratings were good, and I was actually not completely embarrassed by the movie. I especially liked Thea Gill's performance; I'd already enjoyed Thea's work in *Queer as Folk*, and she was equally fine here.

About a year later, my significant other, Ricky, attended a script reading one night. He came home and said, "Guess who was there?

Thea Gill. I told her my girlfriend wrote *Tornado Warning*, and she really wants to meet you."

It took some doing (schedules are hard to match in L.A.!), but Thea and I finally met for dinner, and we had a great time.

A few years later, Brett came to me and said, "You know what I could sell?" (Brett's the hustling arm of our little partnership, in case you hadn't guessed.) "*Coyote Ugly* with vampires."

I barely knew what *Coyote Ugly* was. I think I'd seen a poster or trailer or something. It seemed to be some half-fantasy about a bunch of girl bartenders. Well, WTF...I could write that with vampires.

So Brett and I wrote a script we originally called *Jugs*, which was a play on the fact that our well-endowed vampire women all compared notes about men's jugular veins. The script was almost experimental: It was told in real time, taking place in exactly 90 minutes on the night when our five vamp ladies, hiding out as a traveling rave, are finally tracked down by the cruel master vampire who created them. I wanted it to be fast and fun, to invert a few tropes (the vampires are the heroines!), and to give the tired vampire genre a little feminist zing.

I was exceptionally happy with the first draft. So was Brett. He started shopping it. Through Regent, he'd recently met a producer named Dan Grodnik who was interested in the script. Brett finally came back with a strange offer from Grodnik: He would option *Jugs* for exactly one dollar, but if it went into production we'd get a three-picture deal.

I wasn't completely happy with giving away our shiny new script for a buck, but Brett thought it was a good deal. I finally went in to meet with the producers, and received an amusing surprise:

Dan Grodnik had a partner. His partner was a former actor named Andrew Stevens. In the 1970s, when I was a mere sprite, Andrew Stevens had starred in Brian de Palma's horror film *The Fury*, and I had developed a major teen crush on him; there was something just so hot about a boy with throbbing veins who could blow stuff up just by looking at it. Well, here I was twenty-five years later, talking to my teenaged heartthrob (and I don't mind admitting that he still looked damn fine, uh-huh), and now he was going to be my producer.

Movie number two in the deal was...well, it was a joke. Literally. We'd had a meeting not long ago with Regent to pitch them more disaster movie ideas. Brett and I had cracked ourselves up making up an incredibly silly movie about giant ants taking over a glass skyscraper which we'd oh-so-cleverly titled *Ant Farm*. So we'd been having this pitch meeting whereat we'd pitched five carefully-thought out ideas, and the meeting had just ended up in, "No... no...no...no...no..."

Finally, Brett, in a final frustrated bit of silliness, threw out *Ant Farm*.

It got a yes. On the way out of the meeting, I halfheartedly cursed Brett for now giving us the task of turning a joke into a real script.

Ant Farm was re-titled *The Glass Trap*, and our new producers had a deal with Regent, so they would make the movie. We already had a solid treatment on it, so writing a script would be a breeze.

The third film would be something that Dan and Andrew had been developing. Now, this may sound strange if you're not in the movie biz, but here's the deal: A lot of small movies are sold on the basis of no more than a poster. Yes, really. A poster and a title, maybe with one third-tier star attached. A company will take their poster and promotional materials to a film market like the yearly AFM (American Film Market), and try to score foreign sales just on the premise and the poster.

Dan and Andrew had done this with a movie called *Blue Demon*. The entirety of the premise was this: A scientist creates genetically-altered sharks for the government. They had some existing CGI sharks that they wanted to put to use.

Fine. We could write that. We knocked a few ideas around, and Dan and Andrew seemed to dig where we were going. We got the orders to come up with a treatment. We did. They liked it.

Then it got weird.

"Oh, we have a few other things we'd like to work into the script."

"Okay," we'd say, feeling cocky.

"We have stock footage of two semis racing along a narrow mountain road. We want to use that."

"Uhhh…" we were suddenly feeling a lot less cocky. This was a shark movie. It was all set around waterfronts. Two semis racing along a narrow mountain road?

There was more. "We have a ferry."

Good. We could work in a ferry.

"Oh, but we want to shoot this in Canada, and there are restrictions to shooting in oceanfront areas. But we can get rivers."

Fine. They'd be mutant freshwater sharks. Whatever.

This went on for a few weeks. Soon the river was gone, but they had an indoor swimming pool. The CGI sharks could do some things, but not others.

Well, I probably don't need to tell you by now what happened: By the time the movie was done, it'd been shot in L.A. and had none of those things in it. No ferry, no indoor swimming pool, no chase between two semis along treacherous mountain roads. It turned out to be a shark movie wherein no one actually got killed by a shark (I can assure you that lots of people got chomped in our draft!). It bore maybe a 10% resemblance to what we'd written.

Which put it 9.99% ahead of *The Glass Trap*.

The Glass Trap had also shot in L.A., but I wasn't even interested enough to visit the set (I did visit the set of *Blue Demon*, but only because it was shooting in the former Herald Tribune building downtown, an absolutely magnificent structure built by one of my favorite architects, Julia Morgan). Brett, however, visited *The Glass Trap* and reported back to me.

"What were they shooting?" I asked.

"The scene in the elevator shaft," Brett answered.

I thought for a moment, and then said, "Brett...our script doesn't have a scene in an elevator shaft."

"It does now," Brett responded.

Seriously, by the time this thing was shot and edited, not even character names were the same. The only similarities to anything we'd written were the title and the very basic concept of giant ants in a glass skyscraper. Gone was all the cool science fiction-y stuff we'd done about how these ants had been created in a lab to stop the spread of fire ants, and how they could only be controlled by using certain hormones. Instead, there was even worse inanity about how the ants were atomic or something and could be stopped by DDT.

Brett got off lucky – they misspelled his name in the credits. I was not so fortunate.

But it was the first movie that was the real heartbreaker, the one that'd gotten this whole three-picture deal set up in the first place. *Jugs* had been re-titled *Thralls* (and would eventually be released in the U.S. under the title *Blood Angels*), and this one really would be shot in Canada. I needed a vacation, and thought, *What the hell, I've never been to Vancouver…*

I managed to arrive in Vancouver during one of their coldest winters ever (it was 17 degrees one day when I was there), and they were shooting *Thralls* in an indoor miniature golf course building that was unheated – the poor actresses in their skimpy outfits would huddle in down jackets until the very instant they had to shoot a scene.

Well, the set looked great, the lighting was terrific, the actresses were almost exactly how I'd pictured the characters…

And I recognized absolutely nothing they were saying. Not one word of it.

Fine, I tried to tell myself. The script got a dialogue polish. I could live with that, as long as my feminist message was still front and center.

I ran into one of the lead actresses in the restroom. "Who are you?" she asked. She seemed initially confused when I told her I was the writer, but she warmed up once we chatted for a few seconds. "I love the new draft where I get to turn on the other girls," she said excitedly.

Uhhh…*what*? Well, I did *not* love that. It was crucial to me that the women bond together to survive their ordeal. Having one turn on the others sounded like every other movie ever made with a group of women.

But that was nothing compared to what was coming. As in, the moment when the male villain strode onto the set and said, "Girls, girls, girls, you didn't think you actually did any of this, did you?"

He might as well have been saying that directly to me. My movie had just been castrated. Or whatever the female equivalent is.

My significant other Ricky tells me that the phone call he got that night was the angriest he's ever heard me in my life. I don't remember what I said. I do know that after I talked to him, I walked a block to a great Japanese restaurant, ordered goddamn near everything on the menu and a huge bottle of sake, and got drunk off my ass with some excellent food.

The final insult was when the lab botched my slides from the set. Only the few digital photos came out unscathed. I really haven't shot film since.

I sat through *Blood Angels* twice. The first time was excruciating. Then I watched the trailer, which, weirdly enough, looked sort of like my script, and made me think that maybe I'd misjudged the movie the first time I watched it. I hadn't. It was still pretty bad.

It could have been great. It could have been a movie that people would have watched for years, especially women. And it wouldn't have cost one more dime to shoot it that way. In fact, it would have cost less.

But this is the movie biz, where dreams are bought and paid for and the writer is expected to bend over and take it without Vaseline and be thankful afterward.

Yeah, right. I didn't even make enough money off those three films to buy a new car.

Hooray for Hollywood.

Brett's promotional postcard for *Tornado Warning*

Lisa beats the selfie craze by ten years (using her camera's self-timer) on the Vancouver set of *Blood Angels*

I Get "Tested"

IF YOU THINK THAT SEEING my name on three wretched films that bore little-to-no resemblance to anything I'd written made me even more resolved to stick to fiction, you'd be right.

The abalone hunting trip with my dad couldn't help but inspire a story. I wrote and submitted "Black Mill Cove" to my friend Del Howison for his upcoming anthology *Dark Delicacies*. Even though I'd been friends with Sue and Del for ages – well before they'd set up their world famous store Dark Delicacies and even before they were married – getting into Del's first book was no walk in the park. My competition included the likes of Ray Bradbury and Clive Barker. Del and co-editor Jeff Gelb passed on the first story I submitted to them. But – bless them! – they did indeed buy "Black Mill Cove".

Dark Delicacies was released by Carroll and Graf in 2005. It garnered a lot of very positive reviews, a number of which singled out my story. I'd never received this much critical response to a short story before. This felt just fiiiiiiine.

"Black Mill Cove" also started to pick up steam in the Bram Stoker Awards®, presented annually by the Horror Writers Association. Now just in case you didn't know, I should explain: I've been a pretty key player at HWA for over a decade now. I've been a member, a trustee, a treasurer, a vice president, and finally – after the sad death of the great Rocky Wood in December 2014 – president. I've given far too much time to HWA, but I have a weakness for helping other writers. I really like doing it. It drives people close to me crazy ("how much more time are you going to spend on that?!"), but they tolerate it.

But back to "Black Mill Cove": Throughout the year, HWA's members recommend works for the Bram Stoker Awards (as of 2011, the awards are also partly juried). At the end of the year, the five works in each category that have received the most recommendations move onto a preliminary ballot (along with five works selected by a jury), which is then voted on by the organization's Active members; the five top vote getters then become official nominees. One more vote determines each category's winner.

"Black Mill Cove" finished up 2005 with more recommendations than any other short story. I was kind of floored, frankly. And grateful. But I had no illusions about it advancing past that. Which is good, because it didn't. I think Del was more shocked by that than I was; he still talks about the story that finished at the top of the preliminary ballot, but didn't make it onto the final ballot.

About that same time, I started getting e-mails from friends wondering if I'd seen a new interview with *Cemetery Dance* magazine editor Robert Morrish in which he mentioned me. Me? Why? Well, it turned out that Mr. Morrish had listed me as one of three writers he wanted to work with.

Me?!

Needless to say, I promptly dropped him a note. "I'm here!" I think I brilliantly announced. I sent him a story. He bought it. It appeared in *Cemetery Dance* #55 in October 2006.

The story was called "Tested". On the surface, it was about a man trapped by the wreck of his car on an isolated country road with the enraged thing he's struck (it's implied that this is a

Bigfoot, but I kept it deliberately ambiguous because I didn't want the piece to be remembered chiefly as a Bigfoot story). What "Tested" was really about, though, was how many customers had recently been in the Iliad Bookshop asking for copies of Tom Brokaw's *The Greatest Generation*. I'm going to preface this by admitting that I've not actually read *The Greatest Generation*. For all I know, I'm completely laboring under a vile misconception of it. But from the title and looking at the book and talking to people about it, my impression was that it suggested that those who fought World War II were somehow elevated to the status of "greatest generation". I frankly find this notion completely repulsive. Individuals are great, not generations. And if I were going to choose a "greatest generation", it wouldn't be simply on the basis of fighting a war. How about the generation that came after, the one that campaigned for and largely achieved civil rights? How about the generation that achieved the technical innovations behind the internet? I thought it was bullshit, frankly.

So I wrote about how I felt. In the story, a young man has grown up hearing his grandfather's stories of World War II valor, and wondering how he'd deal with the same situations. And his conclusion, after enduring his own test, is that character is not tested by a mere physical encounter, but also by how the individual processes that encounter.

Whether I've completely misinterpreted Brokaw's book or not, it turned out a lot of others apparently felt the same way I did, because "Tested" received a lot of favorable reactions. It got a few recommendations for the Stoker, certainly not in the numbers "Black Mill Cove" did, though. I was surprised when it managed to just sneak onto the preliminary ballot, then I thought no more about it. I'd long ago decided that I wasn't the sort of author who was ever likely to win awards; I usually think my work straddles a sort of no-woman's-land between too much story and not enough style. As long as a few editors like Steve Jones and Dennis Etchison thought I was good enough to occasionally buy a story from me, that was all I needed.

Those who seize upon any opportunity to denigrate the Stokers (which they enjoy referring to as "the Strokers") will undoubtedly enjoy the symbolism inherent in this next part: I was at the store literally cleaning the bathroom when Del called to congratulate me on being nominated. "Tested" had been voted onto the final ballot.

"You're kidding," I said. I really was completely unprepared, and more than a little stunned. My lifelong self-image as someone who would never be quite hip enough or successful enough or good enough to win awards had just been shattered.

I was a Bram Stoker Award nominee. Wow.

While this was going on, I was working several jobs for HWA. In addition to serving as the organization's treasurer, I was overseeing the awards presentation that year. We would be holding the gala event at the World Horror Convention in Toronto, and I was already working closely with my old friend Steve Jones, who was co-chairing the convention. I was in charge of everything from covering HWA's bills to making sure the engraving was right on the trophies. Yes, I know I could (and possibly should) have gotten someone else to do that, but here's the thing: We'd had a lot of complaints in the past about names being misspelled on both nominees' certificates and winners' trophies. I felt that hadn't exactly added to the Stoker's rep, so I was damned if any misspelled names were going to get by on my watch.

Of course the day came when the final votes were tallied up, and I got an e-mail from the head vote counter, the late Mark Worthen.

Am I giving the results to you? his first e-mail asked. Yes, I told him. I knew that either Mort Castle or Yvonne Navarro or Gene O'Neill or Stephen Volk had won, and any of those names could easily be etched onto the trophy with mistakes.

Congratulations, Mark's next e-mail started.

"Tested" had won.

To say I was stunned wouldn't really be correct; I think "in complete and utter disbelief" would be more like it. Literally; I actually wrote Mark back and told him to re-count, because that couldn't be right.

He assured me the votes had been checked and re-checked. There was no doubt.

Once the realization that this had actually happened had settled in my cranium, there were about three new thoughts that set in: I can't tell anyone until the awards are presented in a month/Is this going to look honest, or will people think I fudged the results?/Will the engraving company think it's weird when the order includes one for me?

The answers, in reverse order: 1) of course the engraving company was fine (they even thought it was pretty cool); 2) I still hope not; and 3) it was really, really hard not to scream it to the world. Most of my friends didn't even realize I was in charge of the trophies; a few figured it out and teasingly asked, which made it easy to just look enigmatic and smile.

Finally the evening of the presentation arrived. At one point Steve Jones and I were alone in the banquet room, putting finishing touches to everything. "So did you win?" Steve asked.

"Uhhh...well..."

"Oh, come on, tell me."

I gulped and answered, "Yeah, I did."

"Well," Steve said, confirming my worst nightmare, "you know how *that's* going to look, don't you?"

"Oh, God, Steve, I know!" I cried out.

Well, I've never personally heard any repercussions to "Tested"'s win...but it bothered me. It bothered me more when I won again next year for Non-fiction (for *A Hallowe'en Anthology: Literary and Historical Writings Over the Centuries*). Here's the thing: At that time, the Stoker rules didn't allow an author to remove their own work or to refuse the award. For any reason. At all. Not even an officer.

I thought that was a crazy rule, frankly. I mean, I understood the reasoning – that the award was for the best work of the year, and if the author had some grudge against HWA, it shouldn't stop us from recognizing the work – but it also, I thought, was close to disrespectful of a work's creator.

So, when a committee to overhaul the Stoker Awards was formed, I volunteered immediately. I was all for moving to a juried system, and especially for giving an author the power to remove their own work.

The committee and HWA's members agreed (for the most part). The move to a partly-juried system was implemented, and the rule disallowing authors to pull their own work was overturned.

About this time, my first novel, *The Castle of Los Angeles*, was published by the wonderful British press Gray Friar. Castle immediately started receiving rave reviews and Stoker Award recommendations.

And I didn't pull it.

Oh, I wrestled with that decision for a very long time. But in the end, I felt it would be unfair to my publisher, who I knew would like to win and who I felt I owed that chance to. I also knew that the fact that the publisher was British might be a nice ideological nod to HWA's international constituency, who justifiably complain that they've too frequently been overlooked in the awards.

So I kept *Castle* in the running, but did nothing myself to push it along (I left that to the publisher, who made electronic copies available to HWA's voters).

And it won (in a tie, with Benjamin Kane Ethridge's wonderful *Black and Orange*). And my publisher was happy. And so were some of HWA's British members.

I'm sure somewhere there was griping. But y'know…awards will always engender griping. After looking at *Castle*'s reviews (it also received a Black Quill Award nomination and made several "Ten Best" lists), I actually thought – at last – that maybe I really had earned this.

But when I took over as HWA's President, I did finally exercise that right to pull my own work. I did that partly out of agreeing with critics who thought the Stoker Awards were too often bestowed on officers, and partly because, frankly, I didn't want to deal with splashback should any of my work win an award while I was in office. It was a kind of cowardice, I suppose, but I'm still glad I took that road. Because God knows, I haven't needed any additional stress during my time as HWA's President.

— 178 —

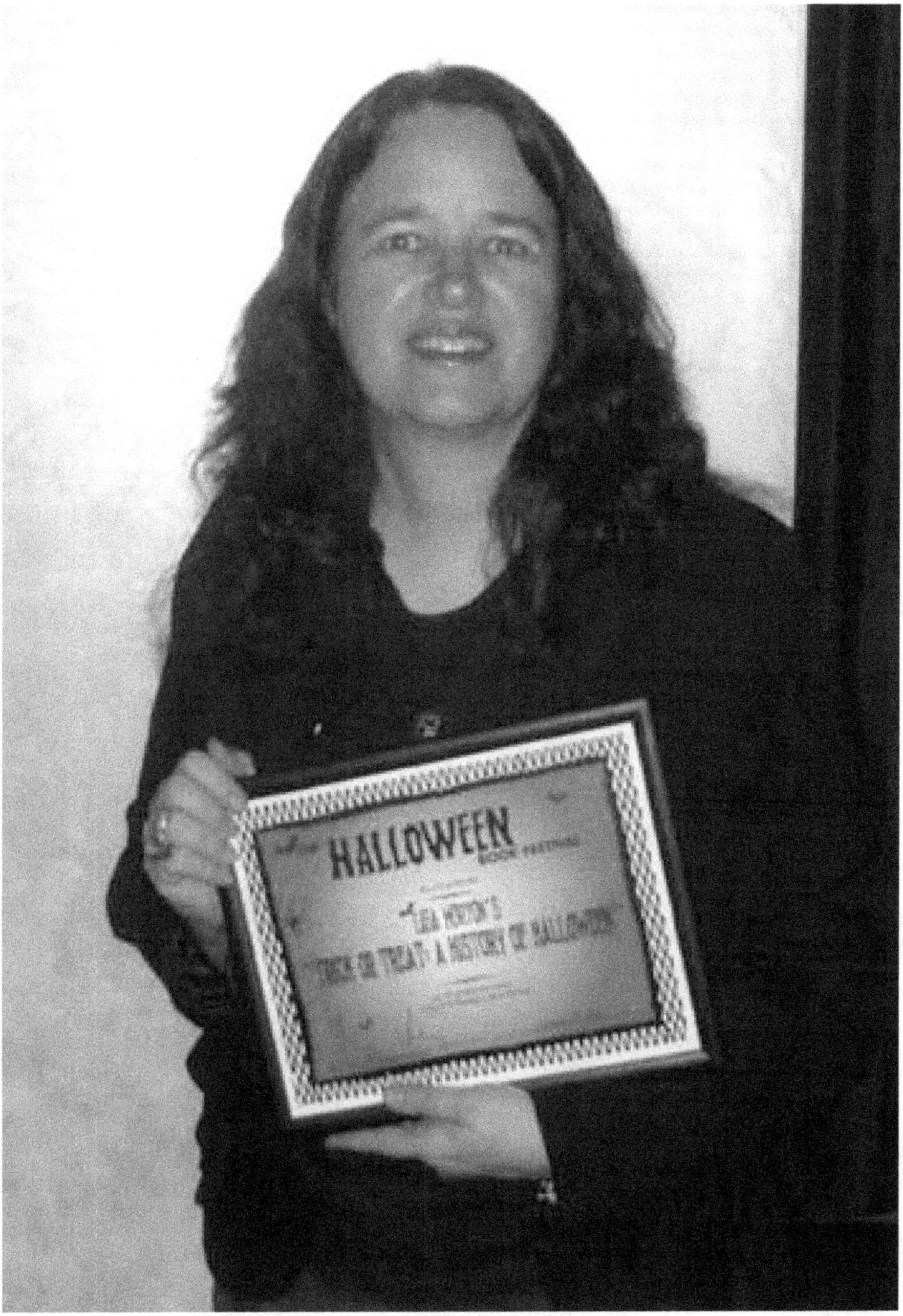
HALLOWEEN

How I Surprised Myself and Became a Halloween Expert

I AM ONE OF THE WORLD'S LEADING EXPERTS ON HALLOWEEN.

It sounds strange to say that. In fact, there's a little voice in the back of my brain screaming, "Do you realize how that sounds?! It's so conceited!"

Well, except for one thing: It's true. I'm the author of two of the definitive reference works on the holiday: *The Halloween Encyclopedia*, now in a second edition, and *Trick or Treat: A History of Halloween*, which received both the Bram Stoker Award for Nonfiction and the Grand Prize from the aptly-named Halloween Book Festival. I've been interviewed on the History Channel and the Blu-ray supplements for the movie *Trick 'R Treat*, on the BBC and Wired.com's podcast "The Geek's Guide to the Galaxy", and I've even been quoted in the pages of *The Wall Street Journal*, *The Boston Globe*, and dozens more.

Beyond mere conceit, though, there's another reason it feels strange to admit all this: Because as short a time as fifteen years ago, it would have been unthinkable. Back in, say, 2000, if you'd told me, "Hey, Lisa, I think you're a world class Halloween expert," I would have laughed you out of the room. It wasn't something I'd ever planned to be, and it finally happened almost by accident.

Of course I've always loved Halloween. I was lucky enough to grow up in a middle-class American suburb during the golden age of trick or treat, and I took it very seriously. I was one of those kids who planned my costumes for months. I was obsessed with authenticity: If I wanted to be a cavewoman, I wore a real animal hide. I spent weeks trying to figure out how to do the creepy eyes of the infected people from *The Omega Man* (hey, I was like ten – I didn't know what contact lenses were, okay?). I loved monster movies and candy and jack-o'-lanterns and costumes.

But so did millions of other kids, and they didn't all grow up to give away years of their lives to the study of the holiday. So what happened to me?

It's like this: Back in 1991, I started working at a used bookstore here in the L.A. area. The bookstore, called the Iliad Bookshop, was only four years old when I started there, but the owner had already built up a clientele and he bought actively all the time. We had a constant stream of old books coming through.

Some of them were about Halloween.

I don't remember now what the first one I bought was, but it was one of the vintage entertainment pamphlets that proliferated in the first half of the 20th century. Halloween, in the 1910s, '20s, and '30s – before the onset of trick or treating – was a major holiday for middle- and upper-class American hostesses who liked to throw parties. Most of these parties were for adults, and the popularity of these parties led to not just an entire new industry catering to retail decorations (Dennison's and Beistle were the major companies), but also created a virtual cottage industry of Halloween-themed party booklets. Most of these little booklets run 100-200 pages, and they have titles like *Handy Helps for Hallowe'en, The Tip-Top Hallowe'en Book,* and *The Jolly Hallowe'en Book.* They often have cute early graphics of witches or cats or pumpkins, and they include everything from suggested menus (one book even recommends foods which are essentially "indigestible" to provoke Halloween dreams!) to party games to decorating tips. They paint a picture of parties that's very different from what we expect now: Back then, hostesses were required to not just prepare a complete multi-course meal, but to provide live musical or theatrical performances, so these little books are even packed with short Halloween plays and songs – there are endless versions of "Jingle Bells" with Halloween lyrics. (These booklets are also frequently less than politically correct, since they come from a time when blackface was still acceptable and racial stereotypes usually consigned African Americans to the roles of easily-frightened, superstitious buffoons).

I soon had a couple of these booklets (there were dozens of them printed), and I had to have more. In 1995, a new website called ebay came online and it was the world's greatest garage sale, with Halloween goods aplenty (and in those early days they were still affordable). One of my first ebay acquisitions was an 1898 booklet called *Hallowe'en: How to Celebrate It*, which I later realized was the first book ever devoted solely to Halloween. At some point I started to buy other books on Halloween, and managed to acquire a nice first edition of the Holy Grail for Halloween book collectors: Ruth Edna Kelley's *The Book of Hallowe'en* (1919), the first hardback book, and a surprisingly good book to boot.

By 2000, I had a nice collection of Halloween books, but it was all just for fun. I had absolutely no intention whatsoever of doing anything with that collection beyond enjoying it.

Then I did my first book for McFarland (*The Cinema of Tsui Hark*), and after it was published they sent me a nice letter asking me if I had any other ideas. I looked at their new catalog, and saw they'd recently published *The Christmas Encyclopedia,* so I sent them a proposal for *The Halloween Encyclopedia,* figuring (very naively, might I add) that I already had so much reference material at my fingertips it would be an easy book to write.

Two years later…

There you have it, then. An innocent interest in collecting quaint old party guides led me to become one of a handful of acknowledged experts on the subject of Halloween. Fortunately, I'm not burned out on the holiday yet. I know there are still more of the vintage booklets out there (although nowadays they tend to be prohibitively expensive), and I'm always looking.

I suppose at this point it's too late to stop.

Who You Gonna Call?

ONE MORNING IN 2011, I woke up to an e-mail that left me so astonished I at first thought it was a joke. It was from a man named Ben Hayes, who worked as an editor at a British publisher called Reaktion Books. I was a big fan of Reaktion's beautifully written and illustrated books; I'd devoured several of the titles in their animal and food series.

Ben was writing to ask if I'd like to pen a Halloween book for Reaktion.

Once I realized this was for real, it took me about another thirty seconds to respond with a big whopping "Yes!" I was offered a decent advance, and set to work writing and collecting illustrations.

I had a great time writing *Trick or Treat: A History of Halloween*, and the book did very well, accruing both sales and awards. Not long after the book was published in 2012, Ben contacted me about doing another book with Reaktion. They were planning a line of volumes on various creatures. They wondered if I'd like to do one.

I immediately wrote back and said yes. I asked if I could have zombies.

Well, it turned out zombies had already been assigned to another writer (as had trolls, werewolves, and gorgons). I asked Ben if he had a wish list of creatures that were still available. He sent me his list. I saw "ghosts" on there, and told him I wanted that one.

I wanted ghosts because of the rich history of ghost stories, many of which are among my favorite horror classics, everything from *The Castle of Otranto* to the works of M. R. James to Shirley Jackson's *The Haunting of Hill House*. I loved a lot of ghost movies, too – *The Uninvited, The Haunting, The Innocents, Ghostbusters*.

Strangely, what I didn't love was the idea that ghosts are real. I'm a lifelong skeptic; I've subscribed to *The Skeptical Inquirer* for years, and I am frequently agog at the strange things people believe. As a nonbeliever, I thought I might be able to bring a unique perspective to the book. I secretly hoped I'd uncover something so inexplicable that it might shake my skepticism. Who doesn't want to believe in the existence of life after death?

As I launched into research for the book, I didn't just comb nineteenth-century documents on Spiritualism and dig through old books on China and Buddhism looking for stories of hungry ghosts, I also set up trips that would take me into supposedly haunted sites.

The first trip was in 2013, when I signed up for an excursion called The Haunted Mansion Writers Retreat. This retreat had been held once before, in 2011, and friends who had been raved about it. It was held at a famed old resort somewhere to the north of San Francisco (I signed an agreement to leave the actual location unnamed, since it caters to many Christian groups and doesn't want a reputation as a haunted house). The building had been constructed in 1911 by a moderately-famed architect, for a millionaire who built the home for his wife. The huge three-story house was set atop a mountain, surrounded by lush forests, a heart-shaped front lawn, and a gloomy, overgrown pool. The house itself was a marvel; it had been remodeled over the years to serve as a retreat, but the ground floor had been kept as a spacious living room, complete with huge windows and overstuffed furnishings. The house was full of nooks and lofts and half-hidden spaces; it creaked and swayed at night, and had a history of family drama and perverse goings-on with servants and even a murder that had supposedly taken place on the stairs going up to the third floor.

The Retreat was organized by a woman named Rain Graves, a striking-looking writer and poet who had worked at the mansion briefly and said she'd encountered numerous ghostly phenomena, including the Holy Grail of ghost encounters: a glimpse of a full-body apparition.

For the 2013 retreat, Rain gathered about twenty writers and artists who would spend four days and three nights in the old building. We'd write, we'd talk, we'd drink, and we'd ghost-hunt. To that end, Rain also invited several professional paranormal investigators, who would arrive on Day Two.

Many of the attendees started reporting incidents almost right from arrival. After the first night, several said they'd been touched while they lay in their beds at night. One, a tempered military man, claimed to have seen a swirling black mass just above his head.

Rain and another attendee, writer Sèphera Girón, were both experienced tarot card readers, and on the second afternoon they led us to a bedroom on the third floor that was supposedly the most haunted room in the mansion, and as we spectators took places around the room, Sèphera and Rain began to lay out their cards, asking questions of the spirits as they did.

Even for a nonbeliever like me, this was a fascinating and oddly beautiful event. Sèphera and Rain were both elegant and compassionate as they slowly turned the tarot cards over, placing them in the time-honored patterns. Stories unfolded as they proceeded; they were conversing with a child spirit who was trapped in the mansion. Watching the two women work was mesmerizing.

We were soon joined by the paranormal investigators, two hip young women, one of whom was a NASA engineer. They set out cameras and EVP (Electronic Voice Phenomenon) sound recorders and thermal sheets to record heat signatures. They set mag lites on the floor, their on-off switches adjusted to react to the slightest touch. As they asked questions, the mag lites sometimes turned on, and then slowly faded out. At one point, an image that looked vaguely like a child's small hand appeared on the thermal sheet. When they played back the sound recordings and bumped up the gain, we heard gruff, whispery voices.

During the proceedings, one sensitive young man panicked and fled the room, convinced he was being pursued by a malevolent entity unleashed by our activities. Screaming ensued. Many of the attendees were too shaken to sleep that night.

I was not among them.

I'd tried to stay open, but was unconvinced by any of the gathered "evidence". I'd seen the slight image form on the thermal sheet, but it could have been anything. The action of the mag lites seemed completely random to me. Where others heard voices murmuring names and warnings on the EVP recordings, I heard blurps of white noise.

I still had a great time at that Retreat (despite coming down with a terrible flu – maybe the ghosts cursed me after all), but I returned home no more convinced of the existence of ghosts.

In 2014, I tried again with another retreat, this time to the Stanley Hotel in Colorado, a venue that – in contrast to my 2013 location – prides itself on its very public haunted history. The

Stanley, located high in the Rockies, hadn't turned a real profit in its entire century-long history until it had begun to tout itself as the birthplace of *The Shining* (Stephen King had conceived his neo-classic ghost novel after spending a night in Room 217 at the Stanley). The Stanley offered ghost walks, ghost tours, and a lengthy paranormal investigation, complete with K2 meters (for measuring fluctuations in electromagnetic radiation), dowsing rods used by an experienced psychic, and various other paraphernalia. Like the mansion near San Francisco, the Stanley is an old, undeniably unnerving structure, with a gloomy, rock-lined service tunnel beneath the building where bodiless voices are often reported, and a separated concert hall that is home to a number of named entities, including a young homeless woman who supposedly crawled into the basement and froze to death there.

I signed up for everything. During the paranormal investigation, which took place for most of an entire night in the concert hall, I handled a K2 meter, sat in a pitch-dark room where my fellow attendees squealed about being touched, and watched the psychic manipulate the dowsing rods. Once again, I was fascinated by the grace and earnestness of the psychic; watching her use the dowsing rods – which are believed to be manipulated by spirits in response to questions – was as compelling as any movie...but, like even the most involving movie, I didn't find myself believing that I was actually watching communication with ghosts. Although the paranormal investigators told us at the end of the evening that it had been an unusually good night for the spirits, I left once again unswayed.

My final ghost-hunting adventure led me to England, surely home to more haunts than any other nation. I took a ghost walk in one of the country's oldest cities, York. I toured Clifford's Tower, the walls of which supposedly run red from time to time with the blood of medieval Jews who died there. In both York and London, I visited haunted pubs and haunted subway tunnels and haunted jails. The most convincing ghost encounter I had in Britain was one I saw my favorite singer, Kate Bush, play a ghost in her brilliant "Before the Dawn" concert. I ended my trip by finally meeting in person my editor Ben.

As I finished *Ghosts: A Haunted History*, though, I did find that my view of ghosts had changed somewhat because of all my investigations. Where I had once been inclined to scoff derisively at any accounts of ghostly interactions, I found I could no longer dismiss them so easily. I'd heard too many people I liked and trusted report ghostly phenomena, I'd seen tarot readers and psychics who were too graceful and genuine to be tossed aside as desperate attention-getters. I had to concede that something was going on, even though it seemed I would never be a part of whatever that something was. I didn't have to believe that the spirits of the dead were trying to contact the living, but I had to accept that my friends and colleagues hadn't simply made up their own encounters.

I guess I became some kind of believer after all.

Calling Doctor Morton

WHEN I WAS A TEENAGER, I went to a science fiction convention where writer David Gerrold was a guest. In my efforts to learn whatever I could about screenwriting, I'd read Gerrold's book on the writing and making of his legendary *Star Trek* episode "The Trouble With Tribbles" three times. I was excited to meet him and get my book signed. Mom dropped me off at the convention, I waited in line, and finally reached the author. I thrust my book at him and blurted out something about how much I wanted to be a screenwriter.

As he signed the book, Gerrold threw back, "Don't do it, kid – there's no money in it."

I was sort of pissed off about that for years. How dare he tramp all over the dreams of an earnest young writer!

Now, all these years and movies later, I not only totally understand what he was saying, I think I could probably go toe-to-toe with him in the cynicism department.

(I do, however, try to be conscientious about what I say to other young writers as a result of that conversation. No point in my destroying their cherished illusions, when Hollywood will do it soon enough anyway.)

After being repeatedly mutilated on multiple levels by agents, producers, directors, and critics, I of course had found my way happily to fiction writing and I thought I was done with

Hollywood. But then, when I least expected it, I was offered something I'd always been curious about but had never been given the opportunity to try before: Script doctoring. Yes, a company I'd worked for in the past was asking me if I could do a quick fix-up job on a script that wasn't working.

Here it was: My chance to do to some other writer what they'd done to me. I could walk all over their script. I could pee on it and claim it as my territory. I could arbitrarily change things, and destroy even the parts that worked. I could make the film more expensive to produce. BWAHAHAHA!! I was drunk on my mad script doctoring power!

Well, of course I didn't really approach it that way (although I remain convinced that some of my scripts were re-written by writers in the throes of that mindset). In fact, what I really worried about was this: What if I read the script and thought it was really good? Would I lose the job by saying, "I'm sorry, but I don't think this is broke and you shouldn't try to fix it?"

Then I read the script. I needn't have worried.

Not only was it awful, it was half the length of a real script. It needed tons of work. There were obvious ways to rewrite it.

Here's where I have to apologize and tell you that you're not going to get any more out of me on this – no hint of title, plot, or even genre, because part of the deal was that the producer would be putting his name on the script. I was happy with that, because I had absolutely ZERO emotional connection to this project, it was a quick turnaround, and the check cleared the bank with no problems.

My company was happy with the script, which has since been shot and which I hear made for a rad little film. I haven't seen it yet, but when I looked it up on IMDB I was pleasantly surprised to see names of characters I'd added. I figure the punch line to the joke that is my screenwriting life is that it'll be the best film I've ever written, and I won't be able to tell anyone what it is.

Whatever; as I mentioned, it went well enough that I got a second gig from it (this time partnered again with Brett Thompson). I'll at least tell you the genre: It was an action script. Or rather…it was supposed to be an action script, but somehow the original writer had neglected to actually add any action. Just a little problem, that.

Once again, it made for an easy rewrite. Our job was to make this thing exciting on a dollar-forty-nine, and keep the overall context of the story. We discussed it in advance, and the producers loved our thoughts on how to make it work. We finished the rewrite quickly, and I even kind of enjoyed the work.

On the day the script was due, I was going over it, making a few final corrections when I got a call from Brett: The producers had just asked for one last-minute change before we sent the script off, just a little something that I could fix in one or two lines.

Sure, of course, I told Brett.

Here it came: Could I turn the fiftysomething, incredibly tough macho hero into a lesbian?

Uhhhhhh…the pronouns alone were more than "one or two lines"…

Well, the good part about that was that it got us one more rewrite pass for a little bit more money. I hear that film has also now been shot.

All I know is that I've got a bunch of fiction deadlines looming before me right now, and that's what I'm focused on. David Gerrold wasn't completely right – I can still make ten times more money off the quickest, dumbest screenplay job than I can off the highest paying short story sale – but it's not always about the money. Maybe that's all he was trying to do – warn one more young writer before s/he waded in with eyes wide and instead got a sock to the jaw.

So, any of you young writers reading this...consider yourselves warned. Now go write something great, and good luck. You'll need it.

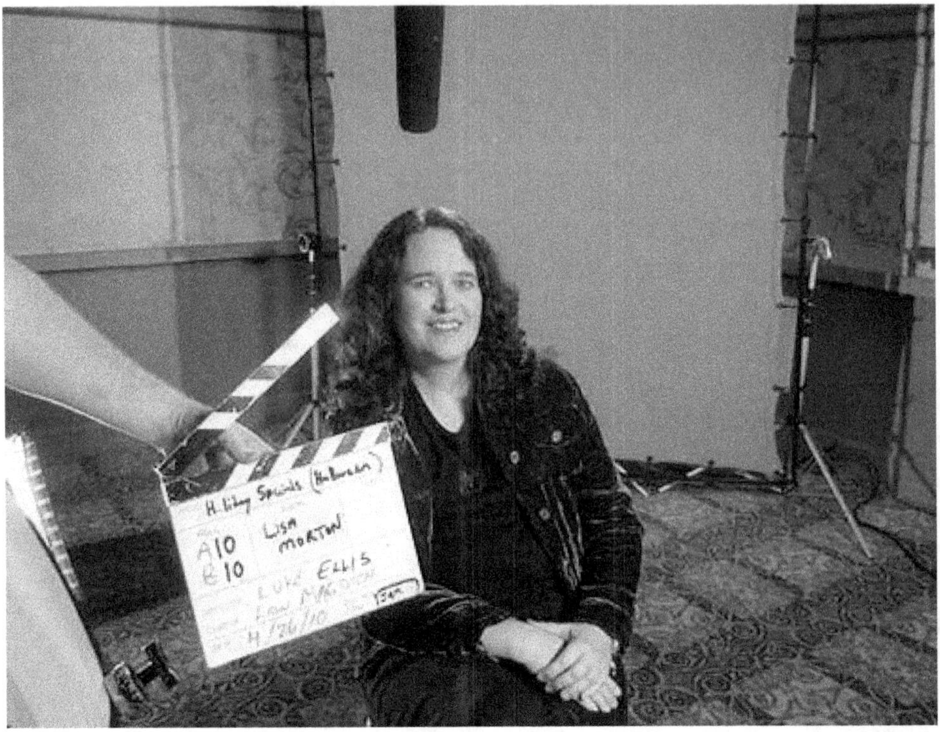
A10
B10
LISA MORTON
ELLIS

Afterword

IT'S BEEN A LONG TIME since some of these pieces were first written...lifetimes ago since they were lived.

My life has changed tremendously since most of the events in this book. This year in particular – 2015 (winding down now, thank God) – has been difficult. Well, I'm not good at offering anything with sugar-coating, so let's just put this right out there: it's been the hardest year of my life.

It started in January with selling one house and buying another; when the dust settled (both escrows closed on the same day, two households had to be packed and moved), I'd become the live-in caregiver to my 82-year-old mother. I thought I was prepared for the job. I'd taken care of my great grandmother throughout my adolescence.

Think of the hardest thing you've ever done and multiply it by five. That'll give you some idea of what it's like to give your life over to an eighty-two-year-old parent.

But that wasn't all of it. On December 1st, 2014, the Horror Writers Associations's extraordinary president Rocky Wood had died, and I suddenly found myself in charge of not just a large and busy organization but also a major event (the 2015 World Horror Convention, which HWA was overseeing).

At the same time, I was struggling to deliver *Ghosts: A Haunted History*, which by January was already long past its due date. I pulled all-nighters sitting crammed in among moving boxes. I'm still astonished that the book makes any sense whatsoever.

And then there were the health problems: 2015 saw my first ride in an ambulance, multiple surgeries, and two months during which I lived on cottage cheese and yogurt because I was unable to open my mouth more than about ½". At least I lost some weight.

But that still wasn't the worst. In May – the same month as the convention – my father was diagnosed with pancreatic cancer. Because he was possessed of amazing strength and fortitude, he out-lasted statistics and predictions, but finally succumbed in early November. I was with him for most of the last week of his life; I spent my Halloween turning down interview requests from his hospital room.

At this point, my writing time consists mostly of whatever I can squeeze in between the time I finally get my elderly charge tucked in for the night and when I can no longer hold my own head up. Most nights I'm so exhausted that I can't manage more than a few hundred words.

But I will continue to manage those words, because I'm not done yet. This week, Random House has made an offer on anthology I will co-edit with Ellen Datlow; the fact that the book is Halloween-themed and would be an official HWA publication brings things almost full circle. For the first time, my name will be on the spine of a book from one of the major publishing houses.

And it's only taken me over thirty years to make it happen.

When I'm asked to give advice to new writers, there's a reason I start with, "Persevere." For female writers, I might tell them, "Be bold," because women are culturally molded from birth to hold back, be "lady-like," let men take the lead. But mainly it's that old saw about hanging in there. Unless you're much luckier than I've ever been, you'll have years of rejections and setbacks; just when you think you've started to make it, you'll find your life turned upside-down. You'll have to figure out new ways to write, whether it's tapping a few paragraphs on your phone during a lunch break or realizing you really can get by on six hours of sleep. But you'll do it, because it's what you live for.

Persevere. Be bold. Try to stay healthy. And someday, you, too, could find yourself looking at a year ahead when you know you won't have enough time to write everything you've already committed to, and thinking, It's going to be a helluva ride.

Fade Out.

Bio

Lisa Morton is a screenwriter, author of non-fiction books, award-winning prose writer, and Halloween expert. Her work was described by the American Library Association's *Readers' Advisory Guide to Horror* as "consistently dark, unsettling, and frightening", and Famous Monsters called her "one of the best writers in dark fiction today". She began her career in Hollywood, co-writing the cult favorite *Meet the Hollowheads* (on which she also served as Associate Producer), but soon made a successful transition into writing short works of horror. After appearing in dozens of anthologies and magazines, including *The Mammoth Book of Dracula, Dark Delicacies, The Museum of Horrors,* and *Cemetery Dance*, in 2010 her first novel, *The Castle of Los Angeles*, was published to critical acclaim, appearing on numerous "Best of the Year" lists. Her book *The Halloween Encyclopedia* (now in an expanded second edition) was described by *Reference & Research Book News* as "the most complete reference to the holiday available," and Lisa has been interviewed on The History Channel, the Discovery Channel's series *Perfecting History*, and in *The Wall Street Journal* as a Halloween authority. She is a six-time winner of the Bram Stoker Award®, a recipient of the Black Quill Award, and winner of the 2012 Grand Prize from the Halloween Book Festival. She has been a guest at the LA Times Festival of Books, the Utah Humanities Book Festival, the American Library Association's Midwinter Conference, and various genre conventions. Her most recent releases are the novels *Netherworld* and *Zombie Apocalypse!: Washington Deceased*. She currently serves as President of the Horror Writers Association, and is also an Active member of Mystery Writers of America, International Thriller Writers, and Sisters in Crime. A lifelong Californian, she lives in the San Fernando Valley, and can be found online at www.lisamorton.com.